THE VIRGIN OF THE WORLD

of

Hermes Mercurius Trismegistus

Translated (with Essay Introductions and Notes)
by
Dr. Anna Kingsford & Edward Maitland

First published 2011
Copyright © 2011 Aziloth Books

All Rights Reserved. No part of this publication may be reproduced, stored in a retrieval system or transmitted in any form or by any means, electronic, mechanical, photocopying, recording, scanning or otherwise, except under the terms of the Copyright Licensing Agency Ltd, 90 Tottenham Court Road, London, W1P 0LP, UK, without the permission in writing of the Publisher. Requests to the Publisher should be via email to: info@azilothbooks.com.

Every effort has been made to contact all copyright holders. The publisher will be glad to make good in future editions any errors or omissions brought to their attention.

This publication is designed to provide authoritative and accurate information in regard to the subject matter covered. It is sold on the understanding that the Publisher is not engaged in rendering professional services.

British Library Cataloguing in Publication Data

A catalogue record for this book is available from the British Library

ISBN-13: 978-1-908388-05-6

Printed and bound in Great Britain by Lightning Souce UK Ltd., 6 Precedent Drive, Rooksley, Milton Keynes MK13 8PR.

Cover Illustration: Diana of Ephesus

CONTENTS

Introductory Essays and Preface		6
Book I	The Virgin of the World	31
Book II	Asclepios on Initiation	57
Book III	Definitions of Asclepios	89
Book IV	The Fragments	99

NOTE

In presenting the "Virgin of the World" - which with my "Hargrave Jennings" Edition of the "Divine Pymander," now so much in repute and demand, are the text books of Hermetic thought - it is no act of supererogation to gratefully acknowledge my appreciation of the valued services of all associated with me in the privileged task of once again reviving those priceless writings of that "Master Initiate," "Hermes Mercurius Trismegistus;" (to be shortly supplemented by the Third Volume, or "Golden Treatise concerning the Physical Secret of the Philosopher's Stone, in seven sections," esteemed one of the best and oldest pieces of Alchemical Philosophy extant; comprising, in epitome, the whole Art, and secret method of its confection, with corroborative annotations from Fludd, Behmem, Vaughan, &c.

Bath; May, 1885.

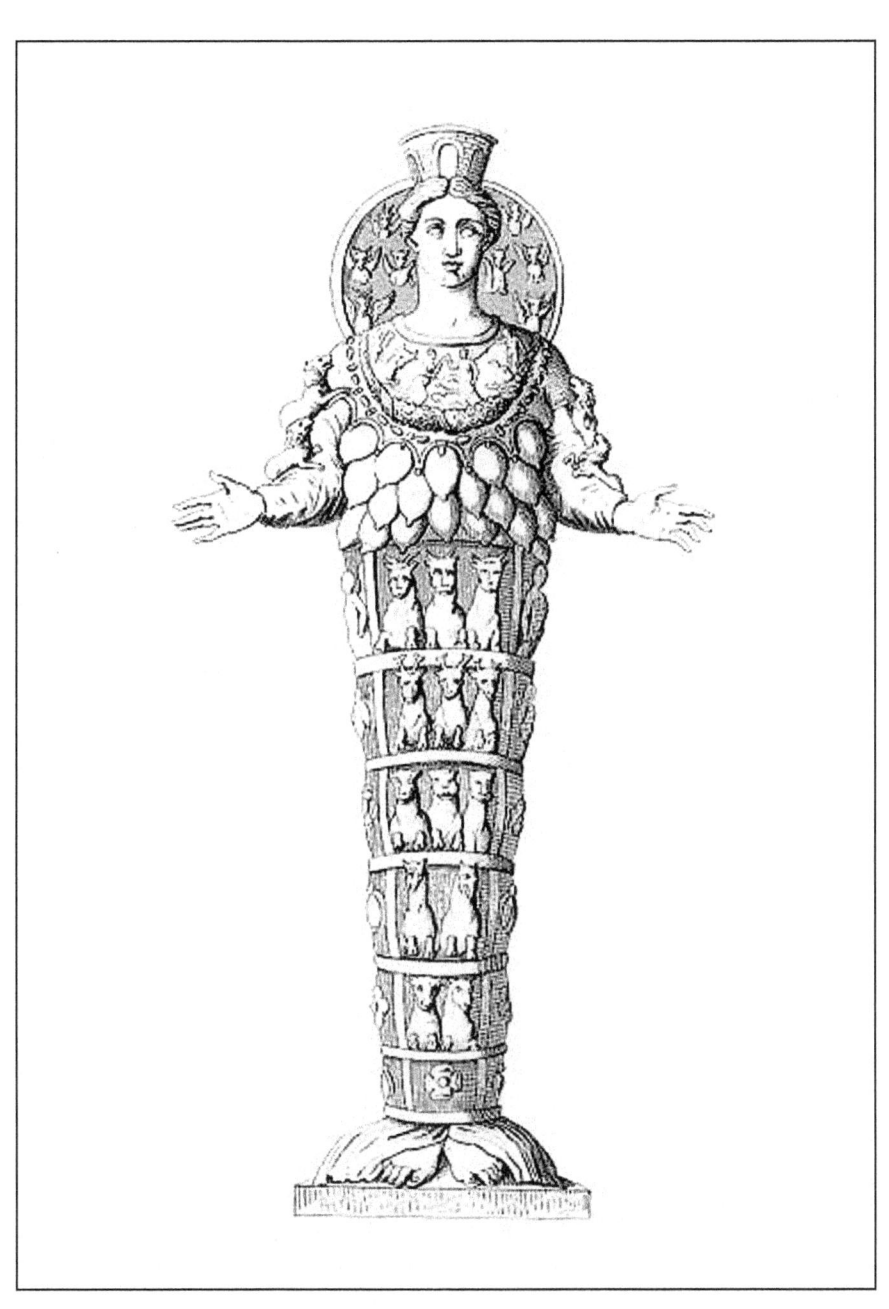

The Hermetic Books

The Sacred Books of Hermes, says Mrs. Child in her admirable compendium,[1] containing the laws, science, and theology of Egypt, were declared by the priests to have been composed during the reign of the Gods, preceding that of their first king, Menes. Allusions on very ancient monuments prove their great antiquity. There were four of them, and the sub-divisions of the whole make forty-two volumes. These numbers correspond exactly to those of the Vedas, which the Puranas say were carried into Egypt by the Yadavas at the first emigration to that country from Hindostan. The subjects treated of in them were likewise similar; but how far the Books of Hermes were copied from the Vedas remains doubtful. They were deposited in the inmost holy recesses of the temples, and none but the higher order of priests were allowed to read them. They were carried reverently in all great religious processions. The chief priests carried ten volumes relating to the emanations of the Gods, the formation of the world, the divine annunciation of laws and rules for the priesthood. The prophets carried four, treating of astronomy and astrology. The leader of the sacred musicians carried two, containing hymns to the Gods, and maxims to guide the conduct of the king, which the chanter was required to know by heart. Such were the reputed antiquity and sanctity of these Egyptian hymns that Plato says they were ascribed to Isis, and believed to be ten thousand years old. Servitors of the temple carried ten volumes more, containing forms of prayer and rules for offerings, festivals, and processions. The other volumes treated of philosophy and the sciences, including anatomy and medicine.

These books were very famous, and later were much sought after for alchemical purposes, especially for that of making gold. The Roman Emperor Severus collected all writings on the Mysteries and buried them in the tomb of Alexander the Great; and Diocletian destroyed all their books on alchemy lest Egypt should become too rich to remain tributary to Rome. The once-renowned Books of Hermes have been lost these fifteen hundred years.

Thus much concerning the Hermetic Books generally.

The Fragments comprised in this reprint have been the subject of much learned research. In the early centuries of Christianity - Dr. Louis Menard tells us[2] - they enjoyed a high repute as of undoubted genuineness, the Fathers invoking their testimony on behalf of the Christian mysteries, while

Lactantius - the "Christian Cicero" - said of them, "Hermes, I know not how, has discovered well-nigh the whole truth." He was regarded as an inspired revealer, and the writings which bore his name passed for genuine monuments of that ancient Egyptian theology in which Moses had been instructed. And this opinion was accepted by Massilius Ficinus, Patricius, and other learned men of the Renaissance, who regarded them as the source of the Orphic initiations and of the philosophy of Pythagoras and Plato. Doubts, however, arose. They were ascribed, variously, on the strength of internal evidence, to a Jew, a Christian, and a Gnostic. And the conclusion come to by recent critics and accepted by Dr. Menard, is that their place is among the latest productions of Greek philosophy, but that amid the Alexandrian ideas, on which they are based, there are some traces of the religious doctrine of ancient Egypt. It was, he says, from the conjunction of the religious doctrines of Egypt, with the philosophic doctrines of Greece, that the Egyptian philosophy sprang which has left no other memorial than the books of Hermes, in which are to be recognised, under an abstract form, the ideas and tendencies which had before been presented under a mythological form.

Another comparison is that which he institutes between some of the Hermetic writings and the Jewish and Christian Scriptures, especially the Book of Genesis and the fourth Gospel, and the works of Philo and the Shepherd of Hernias.[3] "The advent of Christianity presents at first sight the appearance of a radical revolution in the manners and beliefs of the Western World. But history knows nothing of sudden changes and unanticipated transformations. To comprehend the passage from one religion to another, one should not contrast their two extreme terms - the Homeric mythology and the Nicene symbology. It is necessary to study their intermediate remains - the multiple products of an epoch of transition, when the primitive Hellenism, under philosophical discussion, changed more and more by admixture with the religions of the East, which were then confused by advancing upon Europe. Christianity represents the latest terms of this incursion of Oriental conceptions into the West. It did not fall like a thunderbolt into the midst of an old world surprised and aghast. It had its period of incubation; and while it sought a definitive form for its doctrines, the problems, the solution of which it sought, equally preoccupied the minds of Greece, Asia, and Egypt. The ideas were already in the air, which became combined in every kind of proportion.

"The multiplicity of the sects springing up in our days can give but a slight notion of that astonishing intellectual chemistry which had established its chief laboratory at Alexandria. Humanity had put up to competition vast moral and philosophical issues - the origin of evil, the destiny of souls, their fall and their redemption; the prize offered was the dictatorship of consciences. The Christian solution prevailed."

Our critic proceeds to distinguish in the books of Hermes Trismegistus between that which, in his view, belonged respectively to Egypt and to Judea. "When we meet in these books," he remarks, "Platonist or Pythagorean ideas, we must ask whether the author had recovered them from the ancient sources whence Pythagoras or Plato had drawn them before him; or whether they represent an element purely Greek. There is, then, room to discuss the influence, real or supposed, of the East on the Hellenic philosophy. One is generally too liable, on the strength of the belief of the Greeks themselves, to exaggerate this influence, and especially to set back the date of it. It is only after the foundation of Alexandria that a permanent and consistent connection was established between the thought of Greece and that of other peoples; and in these exchanges Greece had much more to give than to receive. The Orientals - at least, such of them as came into contact with the Greeks - appeared never to have had a philosophy properly so called. Psychic analysis, research for the foundations of knowledge and of moral laws, and their application to social life, were things absolutely unknown to the East before the invasion of Alexander. The expression respecting his countrymen which Plato ascribes to the Egyptian priest, 'You Greeks are but children; and there are no old men among you,' might be referred to the East and to Egypt itself. The scientific spirit is as alien to those peoples as the political instinct. They can endure, through long ages, but they can never reach their manhood. They are elderly youths, always in leading strings, and as incapable of searching for truth as of accomplishing justice.

"Initiated into philosophy by Greece, the East could but give in return that which it had, - the exaltation of religious sentiment; Greece accepted the exchange. Weary of the scepticism produced by the strife of her schools, she cast herself, by a reaction, into mystic fervours, precursors of a renewal of faith. The books of Hermes Trismegistus are a bond of union between the dogmas of the past and those of a future, and it is by this bond that they attach themselves to questions actual and living. If they belong still to paganism, it is to paganism in its last hours, always full of disdain for the new faith, and declining to abdicate in her favour, because it guards the depository of the old civilisation which will become extinct with it, already tired of a hopeless struggle, resigned to its destiny, and returning to sleep for evermore in its first cradle, the old Egypt, the land of the dead."

Dr. Menard thus concludes: - "The Hermetic books are the last monuments of paganism. They belong at once to the Greek philosophy and the Egyptian religion, and in their mystic exaltation they impinge already upon the Middle

Age. Between a world which is ending and a world which is commencing, they resemble those animals who by their undecided nature serve as a link between different orders of organisations. These mixed creations are always inferior to each of the groups which they connect together. Not to be compared either with the religion of Homer or Christianity, the Books of Hermes enable us to comprehend the method of the world's passage from one to the other. In them the beliefs which were being born, and, the beliefs which were dying, met and clasped hands."

In contrast to, and also, as we hold, in correction of, the view thus expressed concerning the relative philosophies of Greece and the East, we adduce the following passages from Mr. Plumptre's "History of Pantheism":-[4]

"From our earliest childhood we have generally been taught to regard the Hebrews as those to whom we owe all our knowledge of theology and religion; and in a great measure even our knowledge of God Himself. We have been taught to regard the Greeks as those from whom we have gained all our acquaintance with the arts and sciences, philosophy, and, to a certain extent, all that is comprised within the word wisdom. And in like manner it is upon the Romans we have been told to look as upon those from whom we have gained all our notions of discipline and law. As regards our relations to the Hebrews and Romans, the definition is fairly accurate. Not so with the Greeks. There is, indeed, a certain superficial accuracy about the statement. We do, of course, owe a good deal of our knowledge and learning to the Greeks. But where the definition is erroneous is in this: it leads us to imply from it that the Greeks were the first people who cultivated the love of learning for its own sake; that they gained their knowledge from no other nations, but were the authors of it themselves. It might almost lead us to imply that they were the first people who had ever attained any degree of civilisation.

"The slightest acquaintance with Egyptian or Hindoo history is sufficient to make us detect such an obvious fallacy, and lead us readily to discredit the assertion. The civilisation of Egypt goes so far back in the world's history that it is almost impossible to say when it began. It is almost generally acknowledged now that Moses gained the greater portion of his knowledge from his connection with the Egyptians; and in that case even our first ideas of religion may be traced to an Egyptian source."

Mr. Plumptre goes on to spew that while the Hindoos and Egyptians had long been in possession of religio-philosophical systems of the highest intellectual order, the Greeks were sunk in ignorance and superstition of the most irrational kind, until the occurrence of an event which revolutionised, or, rather, which gave the first impulse to Greek thought, so that in a short time after it Greece sprang from a state of childish ignorance into one in which she became, both commercially and philosophically, the leading power of the world. This momentous event was the opening of the Egyptian ports by Psammetichus, B.C. 670. Previous to that time, the Egyptians had been shut out from all intercourse with Europe and the Mediterranean by an exclusion more rigorous than that which until lately was practised in China and Japan; and Egypt was to the Greeks but a land of mystery and fable, as witness the allusions to it in Homer and Hesiod. But with the system of isolation overthrown which had prevailed for so many thousands of years, the influence of the event upon the progress of Europe was such as to be incapable of exaggeration. First Greece, then the rest of the world, owed their civilisation to it. It destroyed the belief in the old mythologies, and gave birth to Greek philosophy.

There is one respect in which this statement requires modification. The Greek mythologies may indeed have been but irrational fables as popularly received and without the key to their interpretation. But in reality they were symbols denoting, while concealing, profound occult truths. And while their presence in Greece at so early a period shews that colleges of the Sacred Mysteries flourished there long before the rise of Greek philosophy, the identity of the doctrines they symbolised with those of Egypt and the East shews that there had been religious intercourse between these countries long before there was any political, commercial, or philosophical intercourse. Foreign missionary enterprise by no means originated with Christianity. The Sacred Mysteries were continually migrating and planting themselves in new ground in advance of secular civilisation. The migration of Abraham and the flights of Bacchus and of Moses were doubtless all of them events of this character.

Mr. Plumtre's conclusion that whatever there was of coincidence between Greek and Egyptian philosophic thought was due to the recognition and adoption of the latter by the Greeks, is one which it seems to us impossible to escape. And we regard M. Menard's inferences to the contrary as due to his failure to combine with his classical knowledge a knowledge of Hermetic and Kabbalistic methods and traditions. Comprising as do these the world's spiritual history, it is impossible apart from them to form any sound judgment on the matters in question. Those who, enamoured of conventional methods, are unable to recognise any organon of knowledge except the superficial faculties, or any plane of knowledge transcending the range of those faculties, are necessarily intolerant of the idea that there has been in the world from the earliest times a system of esoteric and positive doctrine concerning the most hidden mysteries of Existence, of such a character, and so obtained as to fulfil all the conditions requisite to constitute a divine revelation. Nevertheless, this is the conclusion to which we have found ourselves compelled by sheer force of evidence, at once exoteric and esoteric. It is in Hindostan and Egypt that we find its earliest traces; and if, as assuredly is the case, there are coincidences between the ancient doctrines of those lands, and those of Greece, Judæa, and Christendom, it is because the same truth has passed from people to people, everywhere finding recognition, and undergoing re-formulation according to the genius of the time and place of its sojourn. And this, we may add, is a process which must inevitably continue until man has become either so far degenerate as to lose all care for and perception of truth; or so far regenerate as to attain to the full perception of it, and fix it for evermore as his most precious possession.

But be this as it may, we have seen that even the most destructive criticism is forced to make these three important admissions

(1) That the doctrine contained in the Hermetic books is in part, at least, a survival from the times of ancient Egypt, and therein really Hermetic.

(2) That there is a coincidence between the doctrine which has thus survived and that of Christianity. And,

(3) That this coincidence has been recognised and welcomed by the Church, to the admission that Christianity, so far from being something wholly new and unprecedented at the time of its inception, represents a development from, or re-formulation of; doctrine long pre-existent.

E. M.

Footnotes

1 "The Progress of Religious Ideas."

2 Hermès Trismegistus. Traduction complète; précédée d'une étude sur l'origine des livres Hermétiques. Par Dr. Louis Ménard, 2nd Ed., Paris, 1867.

This translation has been used, but not entirely followed, in the present work, as also have some of the notes, those which are not initialled being Dr. Menard's.

3 A title identical with that of the Pymander, or Shepherd, of Hermes.

4 Vol. I, B. II.

The Hermetic System and the Significance of its Present Revival

To the philosophical student of humanity the most significant and important feature of the present remarkable epoch is, unquestionably, the revival of Occult Science and Mystical, or Esoteric, Philosophy. The significance is due no less to the character of the period of its occurrence, than to that of the subject itself. For the moment chosen has been one wherein the human mind, as represented by the recognised intellect of the age, had become, to all appearance, irrevocably set in the opposite direction - that of materialism. Happily, however, for humanity, such appearance has proved deceptive, as had already been foreseen would be the case by those "watchers for the day," who, recognising the unity of nature, and vitalised on the higher planes of the consciousness, are able to forecast the processes of the mental world by those of the physical. That it is always when the sun is at its lowest point that the day and the year are reborn, is no less true in the world spiritual than in the world material. And while the prevalence of materialism meant the extinction of man's spiritual consciousness, the revival of occult and mystical science means the restoration of that consciousness. History, too, had its lessons of encouragement for them, by shewing that the passing away of old forms of faith is wont to be the prognostic and condition of new and higher manifestations. Hence they had confidence that the Spirit of Humanity, being, as they well knew, real and divine, would, in its own good time, make effectual protest against the extinction threatened; and are able to recognise in the present revival the form which that protest has taken.

The significance of this event is definitely enhanced by the facts, first, that it has brought the Hermetic philosophy into a prominence which it has not known for many centuries; and, secondly, that the revival of that philosophy has been at once the condition and the result of every great religious renaissance the world has seen. For the system designated the Hermetic Gnosis - the earliest formulation of which, for the western world, belongs to the pre-historic times of ancient Egypt - has constituted the core of all the religio-philosophical systems of both east and west, Buddhism and Christianity, among others, being alike intended as vehicles for and expressions of it, though the fact has been recognised by only the initiated few. The great school of scholastic mysticism which was the glory of the church of the Middle Ages, had, although unavowedly, the same basis. This school represented a strenuous and sustained endeavour to rescue religion from the exclusive domain of the historical and the ceremonial, and the control of a sacerdotalism, grossly materialistic and idolatrous, by restoring its proper intuitional and spiritual character. That the endeavour failed to secure a lasting success, and the church of the Middle Ages continued to sink deeper and deeper into superstition, with its usual accompaniment of religious persecution, was due to no fault of the system itself. This requires for its reception, that the spiritual consciousness of the many should have attained a development hitherto possessed only by the few. And the world was not then ripe for a doctrine which represents reason in its highest mode. History thus shows that the revival we are witnessing now, is but one of a series of revivals, all having the same object; and it may be confidently anticipated, that, under the altered conditions of society, the success attained will far surpass any yet achieved. For, gloomy as is the present outlook in every department of human activity, social, philosophical, moral, and religious alike, there never was a time when the conditions were so favourable for a radical and widespread improvement; because there never was a time when new ideas and knowledges found such facilities for propagation, or when, through the intensity of their suffering and discontent, mankind were in so high a state of receptivity. Hence the system has now a chance of recognition surpassing any hitherto enjoyed by it. Having always in the past found exclusive favour with the most luminous minds and noblest natures, it can hardly fail, with due formulation and presentation, to find acceptance with the mankind of the incoming era. Already are there indications not to be mistaken, that the still powerful aid of the church will not be wanting in this behalf, and this no less for its own preservation than for that of religious truth. The world has yet to discern the significance of the action of Pope Leo XIII., in the reinstatement of the writings of Aquinas as the basis of ecclesiastical education. But for the initiates of Hermes this is not doubtful, but affords sure ground for the loftiest hopes. And similarly with that extraordinary, if too often grotesque, phenomenon called modern spiritualism.

From these remarks on the circumstances under which the revival has occurred, of which this series of reprints is at once a product, a token, and an aid; we will proceed to give a slight general sketch of the nature of the doctrine which has played so important a part in the past, and bids fair to do as much, and even more, in the future.

It should be first stated, however, that the materials for our sketch are not restricted to the so-called Hermetic fragments themselves, which form the subject of these reprints. Not only are they, as fragments, incomplete; they are also interpolated and partially corrupt in text, though still replete with the purest and loftiest teaching. Much, too, of that which is genuine is mystical and allegorical, referring to a plane, and needing an interpretation, other than are apparent. Hence, it is necessary for such a task, to utilise the labours of those various exponents of the system who have either derived it from sources not now extant, or who, by following the same method, have discerned it for themselves,[1] giving it, in some instances, fresh applications, not the less Hermetic because representing a further development of the doctrine. No learning or industry, however, can compensate for the absence of that sympathetic insight which alone can detect the characteristic ring of the true Hermetic metal; and which, if hearty appreciation be any guarantee, will assuredly not be wholly wanting on this occasion. At best, however, it is but a slight outline that can be given here.

Starting from the axiom that from nothing nothing comes, and recognising Consciousness as the indispensable condition of existence, the Gnosis, with resistless logic, derives all things from pure and absolute Being, itself unmanifest and unconditioned, but in the infinity of its plenitude and energy, possessing and exercising the potentiality of manifestation and conditionment, and being, rather than having, life, substance, and mind, comprised in one Divine Selfhood, of which the universe is the manifestation.

Regarding all things as modes of consciousness, the Gnosis necessarily regards consciousness as subsisting under many modes, and as being definable as the property whereby whatever is, affects, or is affected in, itself; or affects, or is affected by, another; which is really to say, as constituting the things them-selves. There is, thus, a mechanical consciousness, a chemical consciousness, a magnetic, a mental, a psychic, consciousness, and so on up to the divine, or absolute, consciousness. And whereas all proceed from this last, so all return to this last, in that every entity possesses the potentiality of it. Herein lies the secret of evolution, which is no other than the expression of the tendency of things to revert, by ascension, to their original condition - a tendency, and therefore an expression, which could have no being were the lowest, or material mode of consciousness to be the original and normal mode.

By thus making matter itself a mode of consciousness, and therein of spirit - spirit being absolute consciousness - the Gnosis escapes at once the difficulties which stand in the way of the conception of an original Dualism, consisting of principles inherently antagonistic; and also those which arise out of the kindred conception of non-consciousness as having a positive existence. All being modes of the One, no inherent antagonism, or essential difference, is possible; but that which is regarded as unconsciousness is but a lower mode of consciousness - consciousness reduced, so to speak, to a minimum, but still consciousness so long as it is. Total unconsciousness is thus not-being; and bears to consciousness the relation of darkness to light, the latter alone of the two being, however reduced, positive entity, and darkness being non-entity.

However various the manifestations of the universal consciousness, or being, whether as regards its different planes, or its different modes on the same plane, they all are according to one and the same law, which, by its uniformity, demonstrates the unity of the informing spirit, or mind, which subsists eternally and independently of any manifestation. For, as said in the "Divine Pymander" (B.V.): -

"He needeth not to be manifested; for He subsisteth eternally."

"But in that He is One, He is not made nor generated; but is unapparent and unmanifest.

"But by making all things appear, He appeareth in all and by all; but especially is He manifested to or in those wherein He willeth."

And again: -

"The Essence of all is One."

From the oneness of original Being comes, as a corollary, the law of correspondence between all planes, or spheres, of existence, in virtue of which the macrocosm is as the microcosm, the universal as the individual, the world as man, and man as God. "An earthly man," says "The Key," "is a mortal God, and the heavenly God is immortal man." The same book, however, is careful to explain that by man is meant only those men who are possessed of the higher intelligence, or spiritual consciousness, and that to lack this is to be not yet man, but only the potentiality of man. It avoids also the error of anthropomorphism by defining Divinity to be, itself, neither life, nor mind, nor substance; but the cause of these.

Ignorance of God is pronounced to be the greatest evil, but God is not to be discerned in phenomena, or with the outer eye. The quest must be made within oneself. In order to know, man must first be. This is to say, he must have developed in himself the consciousness of all the planes, or spheres, of his fourfold nature, and become thereby wholly man. It is to his inmost and divine part, the spirit, that the mystery of existence appertains, since that is Pure Being, of which existence is the manifestation. And, as man can recognize without him, that only which he has within him, it is essential to his perception of spiritual things that he be himself spiritual. "The natural man," says the apostle Paul, following at once the Hermetists and the Kabbalists, who are at one in both doctrine and method, and differ only in form, "receiveth not the things of the Spirit, neither can he know them, for they are spiritually discerned," that is, by the spiritual part in man. In such degree as man developer this consciousness he becomes an organon of knowledge, capable of obtaining certitude of truth, even the highest; and from being "agnostic" and incapable of knowledge, he becomes "Gnostic," or has the Gnosis, which consists in the knowledge of himself and of God, and of the substantial identity of the two.

From this it is obvious that what is demonstrated by the agnosticism of the present age, is simply the immaturity of its professors. This is to say, the philosophy of the day represents the conclusions of men, who, how developed soever intellectually, are still rudimentary in respect of the spiritual consciousness, and fall short, therefore, of their spiritual and true manhood - the manhood which belongs to the highest plane. Being to such extent not human but subhuman, and ignorant of the meaning and potentialities of man, they confound form with substance, and mistake the exterior and phenomenal part of man for man himself, and imagine accordingly that to gratify this part is necessarily to benefit the man, no matter how subversive of the real humanity the practices to which they have recourse. Out of this condition of spiritual darkness the Gnosis lifts man, and, giving him the supreme desideratum - which it is the object of all divine revelation to supply - a definition of himself, demonstrates to him, with scientific certainty, the supremacy of the moral law, and the impossibility either of getting good by doing evil, or of escaping the penalty of the latter. The attempt to get good by evil doing only puts him back, making his fate worse. The doctrine of Karma is no less Hermetic than Hindû, the equivalent term in the former being Adrasté, a goddess to whom is committed the administration of justice. In the Greek pantheon she appears as Nemesis and Hecate. They all represent that inexorable law of cause and effect in things moral, in virtue of which man's nature and conditions in the future are the result of the tendencies voluntarily encouraged by him in the past and present. The Hermetic method to the attainment of perfection, on whatever plane - physical, intellectual, moral, or spiritual - is purity. Not merely having, but being, consciousness, man is man, and is percipient, according to the measure in which he is pure; perfect purity implying full perception, even to the seeing of God, as the gospels have it. In the same proportion he has also power. The fully initiated Hermetist is a magian, or man of power, and can work what to the world seem miracles, and those on all planes - physical, intellectual, moral, and spiritual - by force of his own will. But his only secret of power is purity, as his only motive is love. For the power with which he operates is spirit, and spirit is keen and mighty in proportion as it is pure. Absolutely pure spirit is

God. Hence the miracles of the magian, as distinguished from the magician, are really worked by God - the God in and of the man.

A word on the organon of Hermetic knowledge. This is emphatically the mode of the mind termed the intuition. Following this in its centripetal course, man comes into such relations with his own essential and permanent self - the soul - as to be able to receive from her the knowledges she has acquired of divine things in the long ages of her past. But this implies no disparagement to the mind's other and centrifugal mode, the intellect. This also must be developed and trained to the utmost, as the complement, supplement, and indispensable mate of the intuition - the man to its woman. Perfecting and combining these two, and only thus, man knows all things and perpetuates himself. For he knows God, and to know God is to have, and to be, God, and "the gift of God is eternal life."

A foremost Hermetic doctrine is that of the soul's multiple re-births into a physical body. Only when the process of regeneration - an Hermetic term - is sufficiently advanced to enable the spiritual entity, which constitutes the true individual, to dispense with further association with the body, is lie finally freed from the necessity of a return into materiality. The doctrine of correspondence here finds one of its most striking illustrations, but one which nevertheless was wholly missed by the chief modern restorer and exponent of that doctrine, Emmanuel Swedenborg. This is the correspondence in virtue of which, just as the body uses up and sheds many times its external covering of integument, plumage, shell, or hair, to say nothing of its artificial clothing, so the soul wears out and sheds many bodies. The law of gravitation, moreover, pervades all planes, the spiritual as well as the physical; and it is according to his spiritual density that the plane of the individual is determined, and his condition depends. The tendency which brings a soul once into the body must be exhausted before the soul is able to dispense with the body. The death of the body is no indication that the tendency has been overcome, so that the soul will not be again attracted to earth. But it is only the soul that thus returns; not the magnetic or "astral" body which constitutes the external personality.

Such is the rationale of the orthodox doctrine of transmigration, according alike to the Hermetic, the Kabbalistic, and the Hindu systems. It permeates, occultly, the whole of the Bible, and is implied in the teaching of Jesus to Nicodemus, the whole of which, as is also the entire Christian presentation, is, in its interior sense, Hermetic. Not that the new birth insisted on by Jesus is other than purely spiritual; but it involves a multiplicity of physical re-births as necessary to afford the requisite space and experiences for the accomplishment of the spiritual process declared to be essential to salvation.

Seeing that regeneration must - as admitted by Swedenborg - have its commencement while in the body, and must also be carried on to a certain advanced stage before the individual can dispense with the body, and also that it denotes a degree of spiritual maturity far beyond the possibility of attainment in a single, or an early, incarnation; it is obvious that without a multiplicity of re-births to render regeneration possible, the gospel message would be one, not of salvation, but of perdition, to the race at large. What is theologically termed the "forgiveness of sins" is dependent upon the accomplishment in the individual of the process of regeneration, of which man, as Hermetically expressed, has the seed, or potentiality, in himself, and in the development of which he must co-operate. Doing this, he becomes "a new creature," in that he is re-born, not of corruptible matter, but of "water and the spirit," namely, his own soul and spirit purified and become divine. Thus re-constituted on the interior and higher plane of the spirit, he is said to be born of the "Virgin Mary" and the Holy Ghost."

While purely mystical and spiritual, as opposed to historical and ceremonial, the Hermetic system is distinguished from other schools of mysticism by its freedom from their gloomy and churlish manner of regarding nature, and their contempt and loathing for the body and its functions as inherently impure and vile;[2] and so far from repudiating the relations of the sexes, it exalts them as symbolising the loftiest divine mysteries, and enjoins their exercise as a duty, the fulfilment of which, in some at least of his incarnations, is essential to the full perfectionment and initiation of the individual. It is thus pervaded by an appreciation of beauty and joyousness of tone which at once assimilates it to the Greek, and distinguishes it from the Oriental, conception of existence, and so redeems mysticism from the reproach - too often deserved - of pessimism. The Hermetist, like the prophet who found God in the sea's depths and the while's belly, recognises divinity in every region and department of nature. And seeing in "ignorance of God the greatest of all evils,"[3] he seeks to perfect himself, not simply in order the sooner to escape from existence as a thing inherently evil, but to make himself an instrument of perception capable of "seeing God" in every region of existence in which he may turn his gaze. The pessimism ascribed to some Hermetic utterances, especially in the "Divine Pymander," is but apparent, not real, and implies only the comparative imperfection of existence as contrasted with pure and divine being.

It is to this end that the renunciation of flesh as food is insisted on, as in the "Asclepios." Belonging neither by his physical nor his moral constitution to the order of the carnivora, man can be the best that he has it in him to be only when his system is cleansed and built up anew of the pure materials derived from the vegetable kingdom, and indicated by his structure as his natural diet. The organon of the beatific vision is the intuition. And not only is the system, when flesh-fed, repressive of this faculty, but the very failure of the individual to recoil from violence and slaughter as a means of sustenance or gratification, is an indication of his lack of this faculty.

In no respect does the Hermetic system shew its unapproachable superiority to the pseudo-mystical systems than in its equal recognition of the sexes. True it is that the story of the Fall is of Hermetic origin; but it is no less true that this is an allegory, having a significance wholly removed from the literal, and in no way implying blame or inferiority, either to an individual or to a sex. Representing an eternal verity of divine import, this allegory has been made the justification for doctrines and practices in regard to women, which are altogether false, unjust, cruel, and monstrous, and such as could have proceeded only from elementary and sub-human sources.

In conclusion. All history shews that it is to the restoration of the Hermetic system in both doctrine and practice that the world must look for the final solution of the various problems concerning the nature and conduct of existence, which now - more than at any previous time - exercise the human mind. For it represents that to which all enquiry - if only it be free enquiry, unlimited by incapacity, and undistorted by prejudice - must ultimately lead; inasmuch as it represents the sure, because experimental, knowledges, concerning the nature of things which, in whatever age, the soul of man discloses whenever he has attained full intuition. Representing the triumph of free-thought - a thought, that is, which has dared to probe the consciousness in all directions, outwards and downwards to matter and phenomena, and inwards and upwards to spirit and reality; it represents also the triumph of religious faith, in that it sees in God the All and in All of Being; in Nature, the vehicle for the manifestation of God; and in the Soul - educated and perfected through the processes of Nature - the individualisation of God.

E. M.

Footnotes

1 For, as we have subsequently ascertained, "The Perfect Way" is not a singular instance of the recovery of the Hermetic system, by unwittingly following the same method to which it was originally due, namely, intuitional perception and recollection, and altogether independently of extraneous sources of information.

2 The term "corrupt," which in the translation of the "Divine Pymander" is applied to things earthly, means simply perishable.

3 The title of one of the books in the "Divine Pymander."

An Introduction
to
The Virgin of the World

The mystic title of the celebrated Hermetic fragment with which this volume commences, "Koré Kosmou" that is, the "Kosmic Virgin," is in itself a revelation of the wonderful identity subsisting between the ancient wisdom-religion of the old world, and the creed of catholic Christendom. Koré is the name by which, in the Eleusinian Mysteries, Persephone the Daughter, or Maiden, was saluted; and it is also - perhaps only by coincidence - the Greek word for the pupil or apple of the eye. When, however, we find Isis, the Moon-goddess and Initiatrix, in her discourse with Horos, mystically identifying the eye with the soul, and comparing the tunics of the physical organ of vision with the envelopes of the soul; when, moreover, we reflect that precisely as the eye, by means of its pupil, is the enlightener and percipient of the body, so is the soul the illuminating and seeing principle of man, we can hardly regard this analogy of names as wholly unintentional and uninstructive. For Koré, or Persephone, the Maiden, is the personified soul, whose "apostasy," or "descent," from the heavenly sphere into earthly generation, is the theme of the following Hermetic parable.[1] The Greek mysteries dealt only with two subjects, the first being the drama of the "rape" and restoration of Persephone the second, that of the incarnation, martyrdom, and resuscitation of Dionysos-Zagreus. By Persephone was intended the Soul; and by Dionysos, the Spirit. Hermetic doctrine taught a fourfold nature both of the Kosmos and of Man; and of this fourfold nature two elements were deemed immortal and permanent, and two mortal and transient. The former were the spirit and the soul; the latter, the lower mind - or sense-body - and the physical organism. The spirit and soul, respectively male and female, remained throughout all the changes of metempsychosis the same, indissoluble and incorrupt, but the body and lower intellect were new in each rebirth, and therefore changeful and dissoluble. The spirit, or Dionysos, was regarded as of a specially divine genesis, being the Son of Zeus by the immaculate Maiden - Koré-Persephoneia, herself the daughter of Demeter, or the parent and super-mundane Intelligence, addressed in the Mysteries as the "Mother."[2] But Koré, although thus of heavenly origin, participates more closely than her Son in an earthly and terrestrial nature. "Hence," says Proclos, "according to the theologians who delivered to us the most holy Mysteries, Persephone abides on high in those dwellings of the Mother which she prepared for her in inaccessible places, exempt from the sensible world. But she likewise dwells beneath with Pluto, administering terrestrial concerns, governing the recesses of the earth, and supplying life to the extremities of the Kosmos."

Wherefore, considered as the daughter of Zeus and Demeter, Koré is immaculate and celestial in character; considered as the captive and consort of Hades, she belongs to the lower world and to the region of lamentation and dissolution. And, indeed, the Soul possesses the dual nature thus ascribed to her, for she is in her interior and proper quality, incorrupt and inviolable - ever virgin - while in her apparent and relative quality, she is defiled and fallen. In Hermetic fable the constant emblem of the Soul is Water, or the Sea - Maria; and one salient reason for this comparison is that water, however seemingly contaminated, yet remains, in its essence, always pure. For the defilement of so-called foul water really consists in sediments held by it in solution, and thereby causing it to appear turbid, but this defilement cannot enter into its integral constitution. So that if the foulest or muddiest water be distilled, it will leave behind in the cucurbite all its earthy impurities, and present itself, without loss, clear and lucent in the recipient alembic. Not, therefore, without cause is the Soul designated "ever virgin," because in her essential self-hood she is absolutely immaculate and without taint of sin. And the whole history of the world, from end to end, is the history of the generation, lapse, sorrows, and final assumption of this Kosmic virgin. For the soul has two modes or conditions of being - centrifugal and centripetal. The first is the condition of her outgoing, her immergence in Matter, or her "fall," and the grief and subjection which she thereby brings upon herself. This phase is, in the Jewish Kabbala, represented by Eve. The second condition is that of her incoming, her emergence from Matter, her restitution, or glorification in "heaven." This phase is presented to us in the Christian evangel and Apocalypse under the name of Mary. Hence the Catholic saying that the "Ave" of Mary reverses the curse of Eva.

In perfect accord with Kabbalistic doctrine, the allegory of the "Koré Kosmou" thus clearly indicates the nature of the Soul's original apostacy; "she receded from the prescribed limits; not willing to remain in the same abode, she moved ceaselessly, and repose seemed death." [3]

In this phrase we have the parallel to the scene represented in the Mysteries, where Persephone, wilfully straying from the mansions of heaven, falls under the power of the Hadean God. This, perhaps the most occult part of the whole allegory, is but lightly touched in the fragmentary discourse of Isis, and we cannot, therefore, do better than to reproduce here the eloquent exposition of Thomas Taylor on the subject.

"Here, then," he says, "we see the first cause of the Soul's descent, namely, the abandoning of a life wholly according to the Higher Intellect, which is occultly signified by the separation of Proserpina from Ceres. Afterward, we are told that Jupiter instructs Venus to go to her abode, and betray Proserpina from her retirement, that Pluto may be enabled to carry her away; and to prevent any suspicion in the virgin's mind, he commands Diana and Pallas to go in company. The three Goddesses arriving, find Proserpina at work on a scarf for her mother; in which she had embroidered the primitive chaos and the formation of the world. Now, by Venus, in this part of the narration, we must understand desire, which, even in the celestial regions (for such is the residence of Proserpina till she is ravished by Pluto), begins silently and stealthily to creep into the recesses of the Soul. By Minerva we must conceive the rational power of the Soul, and by Diana, Nature. And, lastly, the web in which Proserpina had displayed all the fair variety of the material world, beautifully represents the commencement of the illusive operations through which the Soul becomes ensnared with the fascination of imaginative forms. After this, Proserpina, forgetful of the Mother's commands, is represented as venturing from her retreat through the treacherous persuasions of Venus. Then we behold her issuing on to the plain with Minerva and Diana, and attended by a beauteous train of nymphs, who are evident symbols of the world of generation, and are, therefore, the proper companions of the Soul about to fall into its fluctuating realms. Moreover, the design of Proserpina, in venturing from her retreat, is beautifully significant of her approaching descent; for she rambles from home for the purpose of gathering flowers, and this in a lawn replete with the most enchanting variety, and exhaling the most delicious odours. This is a manifest image of the Soul operating principally according to the natural and external life, and so becoming ensnared by the delusive attractions of sensible form. Immediately, Pluto, forcing his passage through the earth, seizes on Proserpina and carries her away with him. Well may the Soul, in such a situation, pathetically exclaim with Proserpina:

*'O male dilecti flores, despectaque Matris
Consilia; O Veneris deprensæ serius artes!'* [4]

Pluto hurries Proserpina into the infernal regions: in other words, the Soul is sunk into the profound depth and darkness of a material nature. A description of her marriage next succeeds, her union with the dark tenement of the body."

To this eloquent exposition of Taylor's, it is well to add the description given in Homer's Hymn to Ceres. Persephone herself speaks:

"We were plucking the pleasant flowers, the beautiful crocus, the iris, the hyacinth, and the narcissus, which, like the crocus, the wide earth produced. With joy I was plucking them, when the earth yawned beneath, and out leaped the strong King, the Many-Receiver, and went bearing me, deeply sorrowing, under the earth in his golden chariot, and I cried aloud."

Compare with this Hermetic allegory of the lapse of Persephone and the manner of it, the Kabbalistic story of the "fall" of Eve.

"And she saw that the tree was good to eat, and fair to the eyes, and delightful to behold; and she took of the fruit thereof and did eat. . . . And to the woman He said: I will multiply thy sorrows and thy conceptions: in sorrow shalt thou bring forth, and thou shalt be under thy husband's power, and he shall have dominion over thee."

In a note appended to Taylor's Dissertations, Dr. Wilder quotes from Cocker's Greek Philosophy the following excellent reflections:

"The allegory of the Chariot and Winged Steeds, in Plato's Phædrus, represents the lower or inferior part of man's nature (Adam or the body) as dragging the Soul down to the earth, and subjecting it to the slavery of corporeal conditions. Out of these conditions arise numerous evils that disorder the mind and becloud the reason, for evil is inherent to the condition of finite and multiform existence into which we have fallen. The earthly life is a fall. The soul is now dwelling in the grave which we call the body We resemble those captives chained in a subterraneous cave,' so poetically described in the seventh book of 'The Republic'; their backs turned to the light, so that they see but the shadows of the objects which pass behind them, and 'to these shadows they attribute a perfect reality.' Their sojourn upon earth is thus a dark imprisonment in the body, a dreamy exile from their proper home."

Similarly we read, in the "Koré Kosmou," that the souls on learning that they were about to be imprisoned in material bodies, sighed and lamented, lilting to heaven glances of sorrow, and crying piteously, "O woe and heartrending grief to quit these vast splendors, this sacred sphere, and all the glories of the blessed republic of the Gods to be precipitated into these vile and miserable abodes! No longer shall we behold the divine and luminous heavens!"

Who, in reading this, is not reminded of the pathetic lament of Eve on quitting the fair "ambrosial bowers" of Paradise? [5]

From the sad and woful state into which the Virgin thus falls, she is finally rescued and restored to the supernal abodes. But not until the coming of the Saviour, represented in the allegory before us under the name of Osiris - the Man Regenerate. This Redeemer, himself of divine origin, is in other allegories represented under other names, but the idea is always luminously defined, and the intention obvious. Osiris is the Iesous of our Christian doctrine, the supreme Initiate or "Captain of Salvation." He is represented, together with his Spouse, as in all things "instructed" and directed by *Hermes*, famed as the celestial conductor of souls from the "dark abodes;" the wise and ubiquitous

God in whom the initiate recognises the Genius of the Understanding or Divine Reason - the nous of Platonic doctrine, and the mystic "Spirit of Christ." Therefore, as the understanding of holy things and the faculty of their interpretation are the gift of *Hermes*, the name of this God is given to all science and revelation of an occult and divine nature. A "Divine" is, in fact, one who knows the mysteries of the kingdom of heaven; hence S. John the seer, or the "divine," is especially the "beloved" of Christ. *Hermes* was regarded as the Messenger or Angel of the Gods, descending alike to the depths of the Hadean world, to bring up souls from thence, and ascending up beyond all heavens that he might fill all things. For the Understanding must search alike the deeps and the heights; there can be nothing hidden from it, nor can it attain the fulness of supernal and secret knowledge unless it first explore the phenomenal and terrestrial. "For that he ascended, what is it but because he also descended first into the lower parts of the earth?"

With the splendid joyousness and light-hearted humour which characterised the Greeks, mingling laughter and mirth even with the mysteries of Religion, and making their sacred allegories human and musical as no others of any nation or time, *Hermes*, the Diviner and Revealer, was also playfully styled a Thief, and the patron of thieves. But thereby was secretly indicated the power and skill of the Understanding in making everything intellectually its own. Wherefore, in charging *Hermes* with filching the girdle of Venus, the tongs of Vulcan, and the thunder of Jove, as well as with stealing and driving off the cattle of Apollo, it was signified that all good and noble gifts, even the attributes of the high Gods themselves, are accessible to the Understanding, and that nothing is withheld from man's intelligence, if only man have the skill to seek aright.

As the immediate companion of the sun, *Hermes* is the opener of the gates of the highest heaven, the revealer of spiritual light and life, the Mediator between the inner and outer spheres of existence, and the Initiator into those sacred mysteries, the knowledge of which is life eternal.

The panoply with which Greek art invests *Hermes*, is symbolical of the functions of the Understanding. He has four implements - the rod, the wings, the sword, and the cap, denoting respectively the science of the magian, the courage of the adventurer, the will of the hero, and the discretion of the adept. The initiates of *Hermes* acknowledge no authority but the Understanding; they call no man king or master upon earth; they are true Free-Thinkers and Republicans. "For where the Spirit of the Lord is, there is liberty." [6] Hence Lactantius, in his "Divine Institutions," says: - "Hermes affirms that those who know God are safe from the attacks of the demon, and that they, are not even subjected to Fate." Now, the powers of Fate reside in the stars - that is, in the astral sphere, whether Kosmic or micro-Kosmic. And the astral power was, in Greek fable, typified by Argos, the hundred-eyed genius of the starry zone, Panoptes, the all-seeing giant, whom it was the glory of *Hermes* to have outwitted and slain. Of which allegory the meaning is, that they who have the Hermetic secret are not subject to Fate, but have passed beyond the thrall of metempsychosis, and have freed themselves from "ceaseless whirling on the wheel" of Destiny. To know God is to have overcome death, and the power of death. To know the origin and secret of delusion is to transcend delusion.

The spheres of delusion, dominated by the sevenfold astral Powers, lie between the Soul and God. Beyond these spheres are the celestial "Nine Abodes," wherein, say the Mysteries, Demeter vainly sought the lost Persephone. For from these abodes she had lapsed into a mundane and material state, and thereby had fallen under the power of the planetary rulers; that is, of Fate, personified by Hekate. On the tenth day, therefore, the divine Drama shows Demeter meeting the Goddess of Doom and Retribution, the terrible Hekate Triformis - personification of Karma - by whom the "Mother" is told of Persephone's abduction and detention in the Hadean world. And - we learn - Hekate becomes thereafter the constant attendant of Persephone. All this is, of course, pregnant with the deepest significance. Until the Soul falls into Matter, she has no Fate, or Karma. Fate is the appanage and result of Time and of Manifestation. In the sevenfold astral spheres the Moon is representative of Fate, and presents two aspects, the benign and the malignant. Under the benign aspect the Moon is Artemis, reflecting to the Soul the divine light of Phœbos; under the malignant aspect she is Hekate the Avenger, dark of countenance; and three beaded, being swift as a horse, sure as a dog, and as a lion implacable. She it is who, fleet, sagacious, and pitiless, hunts guilty souls from birth to birth, and outwits death itself with unerring justice. To the innocent and chaste soul, therefore, the lunar power is favorable. Artemis is the patron and protectress of virgins - that is, of souls undefiled with the traffic of Matter. In this aspect the Moon is the Initiatrix, Isis the Enlightener, because through a beneficent Karma, or fate, the soul receives interior illumination, and the dark recesses of her chamber are lit up by sacred reminiscences. Hence, in subsequent births, such a soul becomes prophetic and "divine." But to the corrupt and the evil-hearted the influence of the Moon is malignant, for to such she assumes the aspect of Hekate, smiting by night, and terrifying with ghostly omens of misfortune. These souls fear the lunar power, and in this instinctive dread may be discerned their secret recognition of the evil fate which they are preparing for themselves in existences to come. The Tree of Good and Evil, says the Kabbala, has its root in Malchuth - the Moon.

It has been sometime asserted that the doctrine of Karma is peculiar to Hindu theology. On the contrary, it is clearly exhibited alike in the Hebrew, Hellenic, and Christian Mysteries. The Greeks called it Fate; the Christians know it as Original Sin. With which sin all mortal men come into the world, and on account of which all pass under condemnation. Only the "Mother of God" is exempt from it, the "virgin immaculate," through whose Seed the world shall be redeemed.

"As the lily among the thorns," sings the Church in the "Office of the Immaculate Conception," "so is the Beloved among the Daughters of Adam. Thou art all fair, O Beloved, and the original stain is not in thee: Thy name, O Mary, is as oil poured out; therefore, the virgins love thee exceedingly."

If, then, by Persephone or Koré, the "Virgin of the World," we are thus plainly taught to understand the Soul, we are no less plainly taught to see in Isis, the Initiatrix or Enlightener. Herself, equally with Koré, virgin and mother, the Egyptian Isis is, in her philosophical aspect, identical with the Ephesian Artemis, the Greek personification of the fructifying and all-nourishing power of Nature. She was regarded as the "inviolable and perpetual Maid of heaven;" her priests were eunuchs, and her image in the magnificent temple of Ephesus represented her with many breasts.[7] In works of art Artemis appears variously, as the huntress, accompanied by hounds, and carrying the implements of the chase; as the Goddess of the Moon, covered with a long veil reaching to her feet, and her head adorned with a crescent; or as the many-breasted Mother-Maid, holding a lighted torch in her hand. The Latins worshipped her under the name of Diana, and it is as Diana that the Ephesian Artemis is mentioned in the Acts of the Apostles. Isis had all the attributes ascribed to the lunar divinity of the Greeks and Romans; and hence, like Artemis and Diana, she was identified with the occult principle of Nature - that is, Fate, which in its various aspects and relations was severally viewed as Fortune, Retribution, Doom, or Destiny; a principle represented, as we have already seen, by the Kabbalists, under the figure of Malchuth, or the Moon; and by the Hindu theosophists under the more abstract conception of Karma. The hounds of Artemis, or Diana, are the occult powers which hunt down and pursue the soul from birth to birth; the inevitable, implacable forces of Nature which, following evermore on the steps of every ego, compel it into the conditions successively engendered by its actions, as effect by cause. Hence Actæon, presuming upon Fate, and oblivious of the sanctity and inviolability of this unchanging law of Karmic Destiny, is torn in pieces by his own dogs, to wit, his own deeds, which by the decree of the implacable Goddess, turn upon and rend him. So also, in accordance with this philosophical idea, those who were initiated into the mysteries of Isis, wore in the public processions masks representing the heads of dogs. So intimately was the abstract conception of the moon associated by the ancients with that of the secret influence and power of Destiny in Nature, that Proclos in his Commentary upon the Timæus says of Diana: - "She presides over the whole of the generation into natural existence, leads forth into light all natural reasons, and extends a prolific power from on high even to the subterranean realms." These words completely describe the Egyptian Isis, and show us how the moon, occultly viewed as the Karmic power, was regarded as the cause of continued generation in natural conditions, pursuing souls even into the Hadean or purgatorial spheres and visiting upon them the fruition of their past. Hence, too, in the Orphic Hymn to Nature, that Goddess is identified with Fortune, and represented as standing with her feet upon a wheel which she continually turns, - "moving with rapid motion on an eternal wheel." And again, in another Orphic Hymn, Fortune herself is invoked as Diana. Proclos, in the Commentary to which reference has already been made, declares that "the moon is the cause of Nature to mortals, and the self-revealing image of the Fountain of Nature." "If," says Thomas Taylor, "the reader is desirous of knowing what we are to understand by the fountain of Nature of which the moon is the image, let him attend to the following information, derived from a long and deep study of the ancient theology, for from hence I have learned that there are many divine fountains contained in the essence of the Demiurgus of the world; and that among these there are three of a very distinguished rank, namely, the fountain of souls, or Juno (Hera), the fountain of virtues, or Minerva (Athena), and the fountain of nature, or Diana (Artemis). . . . And this information will enable us to explain the meaning of the following passages in Apuleius, the first of which is in the beginning of the eleventh book of his Metamorphoses, wherein the divinity of the moon is represented as addressing him in this sublime manner: - 'Behold, Lucius, moved with thy supplications, I am present; I, who am Nature, the parent of things, mistress of all the elements, initial progeny of the ages, the highest of the divinities, queen of departed spirits, the first of the celestials, of Gods and Goddesses the sole likeness of all; who rule by my nod the luminous heights of the heavens, the salubrious breezes of the sea, and the woful silences of the infernal regions, and whose divinity, in itself but one, is venerated by all the earth, in many characters, various rites, and different appellations. . . Those who are enlightened by the emerging rays of the rising sun, the Æthiopians and Aryans, and likewise the Egyptians, powerful in ancient learning, who reverence my divinity with ceremonies perfectly appropriate, call me by my true appellation Queen Isis.' And again, in another place of the same book, he says of the moon: - 'The supernal Gods reverence thee, and those in the realms beneath do homage to thy divinity. Thou dost make the world to revolve, and the sun to illumine, thou rulest the universe and treadest on Tartarus. To thee the stars respond, the deities rejoice, time returns by thee, the elements give thee service.' For all this easily follows if we consider it as spoken of the fountain-deity of Nature subsisting in the Demiurgus, and which is the exemplar of that nature which flourishes in the lunar orb and throughout the material world."

Thus enlightened as to the office and functions of Isis, we are at no loss to understand why she is selected by the writer of the following Hermetic fragment as the exponent of the origin, history, and destiny of the soul. For she is, in a peculiar sense, the arbiter of the soul's career in existence, her guardian and overseer. If Demeter, the Divine Intelligence, be the Mother of Koré, then Isis is her foster-mother, for no sooner does the soul fall into generation than Isis becomes her directress and the dispenser of her fate. It is not surprising, therefore, to find that by some mythologists Isis is identified with Demeter, and the sufferings of the former modified accordingly, to harmonise with the allegory of the sorrows of Demeter as set forth in the Eleusinian Mysteries. But the cause of this confusion is obvious to those who rightly understand the Hermetic method. Isis, whether as Artemis (Good Fortune), or as Hekate (Evil Fortune), is the controlling and illuminating influence of the soul while remaining within the jurisdiction of Nature and Time; Demeter, the Divine Intelligence, represents the heavenly fountain or super-mundane source, whence the soul originally draws her being, and as such, is concerned directly, not with her exile and wanderings in material conditions, but with her final recovery from generation and return to the celestial abodes. Consistently with this idea, Isis is represented sometimes as the spouse, sometimes as the mother of Osiris, the Saviour of men. For Osiris is the microcosmic sun, the counterpart in the human system of the macrocosmic Dionysos or Son of God. So that those authors who confound Isis with Demeter, equally and quite comprehensibly confound Osiris with Dionysos, and regard the former as the central figure of the Bacchic Mysteries. The Hermetic books admit three expressions of Deity: first, the supreme, abstract, and infinite God, eternally self-subsistent and unmanifest; secondly, the only-Begotten, the manifestation of Deity in the universe; thirdly, God in man, the Redeemer, or Osiris. On one of the walls of the Temple of the Sun at Philae, and on the gate of that at Medinet-Abou are inscribed these words: - "He has made all that is, and without Him nothing that is hath been made," words which, fourteen centuries or more afterwards, were applied by the writer of S. John's Gospel to the Word of God. The micro-cosmic Sun, or Osiris, was the image and correspondence of this macrocosmic Sun; the regenerating principle within the man, begotten by means of the soul's experience in Time and Generation. And hence the intimate association between this regenerating principle by which the redemption of the individual was effected, and the divine power in Nature, personified by Isis, whose function it was to minister to that redemption by the ordination of events and conditions appropriate to the soul's development. Isis is thus the secret motive-power of Evolution; Osiris is the ultimate ideal Humanity towards the realisation of which that Evolution moves.

     A.K.

Footnotes

1 Dr. Wilder, in his Introduction to the work of Mr. Thomas Taylor, the Platonist, entitled "Dissertation on the Eleusinian Mysteries," asserts that the name Koré is also Sanscrit, and that the Hindu goddess Parasu-pani, also called Gorée, is identical with the Koré-Persephoneia of Hellenic worship.

2 The Spirit, under the name of Atman, is the chief topic of Hindu esoteric philosophy, the Upanishads being exclusively devoted to it. They ascribe to Atman the qualities of self-subsistence, unity, universality, immutability, and incorruptibility. It is independent of Karma, or acquired character and destiny, and the full knowledge of it redeems from Karma the personality informed of it. Atman is also the all-seeing; and, as the Mantras say, He who recognises the universe in his own Atman, and his own Atman in the universe, knows no hatred.

3 I substitute the singular for the plural number, but this alters nothing in the sense.

4 *'O flowers fatally clear, and the mother's counsels despised!*
O cruel arts of crafty Venus!'

5 Milton's "Paradise Lost," Book XI.

6 "Follow no man," said John Inglesant's adviser - "there is nothing in the world of any value but the Divine Light - follow it."

7 The many-breasted figure which forms the frontispiece of this volume, represents Isis under this aspect. The black face and hands are, of course, equivalent to the celebrated Veil, and indicate the inscrutable nature of the occult influence which directs Destiny; and which, to the uninitiate, even appears to be blind and fortuitous. The well-known "black virgin" has the same significance.

BOOK I
THE VIRGIN
OF THE WORLD

PART I.

Having thus spoken, Isis first pours out for Horos the sweet draught of immortality which souls receive from the Gods, and thus begins the most holy discourse.

Heaven, crowned with stars, is placed above universal nature, O my son Horos, and nothing is wanting to it of that which constitutes the whole world. It is necessary, then, that all nature should be adorned and completed by that which is above her, for this Order could not proceed from below to above. The supremacy of the greater mysteries over the lesser is imperative. Celestial order reigns over terrestrial order, as being absolutely determined, and inaccessible to the idea of death. Wherefore, the things below lament, being filled with fear before the marvellous beauty and eternal permanence of the heavenly world. For, indeed, a spectacle worthy of contemplation and desire were these magnificences of heaven, revelations of the God as yet unknown, and this sumptuous majesty of night illumined with a penetrating radiance, albeit less than that of the sun, and all these other mysteries which move above in harmonious cadence, ruling and maintaining the things below by secret influences. And so long as the Universal Architect refrained from putting an end to this incessant fear, to these anxious investigations, ignorance enveloped the universe. But when He judged good to reveal Himself to the world, He breathed into the Gods the enthusiasm of love, and poured into their mind the splendour which His bosom contained, that they might first be inspired with the will to seek, next with the desire to find, and lastly with the power to readjust.

Now, my wondrous child Horos, all this could not happen among mortals, for as yet they did not exist; but it took place in the universal Soul in sympathy with the mysteries of heaven. This was Hermes, the Kosmic Thought. He beheld the universe of things, and having seen, he understood, and having understood, he had the power to manifest and to reveal. That which he thought, he wrote; that which he wrote, he in great part concealed, wisely silent. and speaking by turns, so that while the world should last, these things might be sought. And thus, having enjoined upon the Gods, his brethren, that they should follow in his train, he ascended to the stars. But he had for successor his son, and the heir of his knowledges, Tat, and a little later, Asclepios, son of Imouthè, by the counsels of Pan and Hephaistos, and all those for whom sovereign Providence reserved an exact knowledge of heavenly things.

Hermes then justified himself in the presence of those who surrounded him, in that he had not delivered the integral theory to his son, on account of his youth. But I, having arisen, beheld with mine eyes, which see the invisible secrets of the beginnings of things,[1] and at length, but with certainty, I understood that the sacred symbols of the Kosmic elements were hidden near the secrets of Osiris. Hermes returned to heaven, having pronounced an invocatory speech.

It is not fitting, O my Son, that this recital be left incomplete; thou must be informed of the words of Hermes when he laid down his books. "O sacred books," he said, "of the Immortals, ye in whose pages my hand has recorded the remedies by which incorruptibility is conferred, remain for ever beyond the reach of destruction and of decay, invisible and concealed from all who frequent these regions, until the day shall come in which the ancient heaven shall bring forth instruments worthy of you, whom the Creator shall call souls."

Having pronounced upon his books this invocation, he wrapped them in their coverings, returned into the sphere which belonged to him, and all remained hidden for a sufficient space.

And Nature, O my Son, was barren until the hour in which those who are ordained to survey the heavens, advancing towards God, the King of all things, deplored the general inertia, and affirmed the necessity of setting forth the universe. No other than Himself could accomplish this work.

"We pray Thee," said they, "to consider that which already is, and that which is necessary for the future."

At these words, the God smiled benignant, and commanded Nature to exist. And, issuing with His voice, the *Feminine* came forth in her perfect beauty. The Gods with amaze beheld this marvel. And the great Ancestor, pouring out for Nature an elixir, commanded her to be fruitful; and forthwith, penetrating the universe with His glance, He cried, "Let heaven be the plenitude of all things, and of the air, and of the ether." God spake, and it was done. But Nature, communing with herself, understood that she might not transgress the commandment of the Father, and, uniting herself to Labour, she produced a most beautiful daughter, whom she called Invention, and to whom God accorded being.

And having differentiated created forms, He filled them with mysteries, and gave the command of them to Invention.

Then, not willing that the upper world should be inactive, He saw fit to fill it with spirits, in order that no region should remain in immobility and inertia; and in the accomplishment of His work He used His sacred art. For, taking of Himself such essence as was necessary, and mingling with it an intellectual flame, He combined with these other materials by unknown ways. And having achieved by secret formulas the union of these principles, He endowed with motion the universal combination. Gradually, in the midst of the protoplasm, glittered a substance more subtle, purer, more limpid, than the elements from which it was generated. It was transparent, and the Artist alone perceived it. Soon, it attained its perfection, being neither melted by the fire, nor chilled by the breath, but possessing the stability of a special combination, and having its proper type and constitution. He bestowed on it a happy name, and, according to the similitude of its energies, He called it Self-Consciousness.

Of this product he formed myriads of Souls, employing the choicest part of the mixture for the end which He had in view, proceeding with order and measure, according to His knowledge and His reason. The souls were not necessarily different, but the choicest part, animated by the Divine motion, was not identical with the rest. The first layer was superior to the second, more perfect and pure; the second, inferior truly to the first, was superior to the third; and thus, until sixty degrees, was completed the total number. Only, God established this law, that all equally should be eternal, being of one essence, whose forms He alone determines. He traced the limits of their sojourn on the heights of nature, so that they might turn the wheel according to the laws of Order and of wise discretion, for the joy of their Father.

Then, having summoned to these splendid regions of ether the souls of every grade, He said to them: "O souls, beautiful children of my breath and of my care, you whom I have produced with my hands, in order to consecrate you to my universe, hear my words as a law: - Quit not the place assigned to you by my will. The abode which awaits you is heaven, with its galaxy of stars and its thrones of virtue. If you attempt any transgression against my decree, I swear by my sacred breath, by that elixir of which I formed you, and by my creative hands, that I will speedily forge for you chains and cast you into punishment."

Having thus spoken, God, my Master, mingled together the rest of the congenial elements, earth and water, and pronouncing certain powerful and mystic words - albeit different from the first - He breathed into the liquid protoplasm motion and life, rendered it thicker and more plastic, and formed of it living beings of human shape. That which remained He gave to the loftiest souls inhabiting the region of the Gods in the neighbourhood of the stars, who are called the Sacred Genii. "Work," said He, "my children, offspring of my nature; take the residue of my task, and let each one of you make beings in his image. I will give you models."

Therewith He took the Zodiac and ordained the world in conformity with -vital movements, placing the animal signs after those of human form. And after having given forth the creative forces and generative breath for the whole range of beings yet to come, He withdrew, promising to unite to every visible work an invisible breath and a reproductive principle, so that each being might engender its similar without necessity to create continually new entities. [2]

And what did the souls do, O my Mother?

And Isis answered: - They took the mingled material, O my Son Horos, and began to reflect thereon, and to adore this combination, the work of the Father. Next, they sought to discover of what it was composed, which, indeed, it was not easy to find. Then, fearing that this search might excite the anger of the Father, they set themselves to carry out His commands. Therefore, taking the upper portion of the protoplasm, that which was lightest, they created of it the race of birds. The compound having now become more compact and assuming a denser consistency, they formed of it the quadrupeds; while of the thickest part which needed a moist vehicle for its support, they made fishes. The remainder, being cold and heavy, was employed by the souls in the creation of reptiles.

Forthwith, O my Son, proud of their work, they were not afraid to transgress the Divine law, and, in spite of the prohibition, they receded from their appointed limits. Not willing to remain longer in the same abode, they moved ceaselessly, and repose seemed to them death.[3]

But, O my Son - (thus Hermes informed me) - their conduct could not escape the eye of the Lord God of all things; He minded to punish them, and to prepare for them hard bonds. The Ruler and Master of the universe resolved then for the penance of the souls, to mould the human organism, and having called me to Him, said Hermes, He spoke in this wise: - "O soul of my soul, holy thought of my thought, how long shall earthly Nature remain sad? How long shall the creation already produced continue inactive and without praise? Bring hither before me all the Gods of heaven."

Thus God spake, quoth Hermes, and all obeyed His decree. "Look upon the earth," He said to them, "and upon all things beneath,"

Straightway they looked, and understood the will of the Lord. And when He spoke to them of the creation of Man, asking of each what he could bestow upon the race about to be born, the Sun first replied: - "I will illumine mankind." Then the Moon promised enlightenment in her turn, adding that already she had created Fear, Silence, Sleep, and Memory. Kronos announced that he had begotten Justice and Necessity. Zeus said, "In order to spare the future race perpetual wars, I have generated Fortune, Hope, and Peace." Ares declared himself already father of Conflict, impetuous Zeal, and Emulation, Aphrodite did not wait to be called upon: "As for me, O Master," she said, "I will bestow upon mankind Desire, with voluptuous Joy and Laughter, that the penalty, to which our sister Souls are destined may not weigh on them too hardly." These words of Aphrodite, O my Son, were welcomed gladly. "And I," said Hermes, "will endow human nature with Wisdom, Temperance, Persuasion, and Truth; nor will I cease to ally myself with Invention. I will ever protect the mortal life of such men as are born under my signs, seeing that to me the Creator and Father has attributed in the Zodiac, signs of Knowledge and Intelligence; above all, when the movement which draws thereto the stars is in harmony with the physical forces of each." [4]

He Who is Master of the world rejoiced at hearing these things, and decreed the production of the human race. As for me - said Hermes - I sought what material ought to be employed in the work, and invoked the Lord. He commanded the Souls to give up the residue of the protoplastic substance, which having taken, I found it entirely dried up. Therefore, I used a great excess of water wherewith to renew the combination of the substance, in such wise that the product might be resolvable, yielding, and feeble, and that Force should not be added therein to Intelligence. When I had achieved my work it was beautiful, and I rejoiced in seeing it. And from below I called upon the Lord to behold what I had done. He saw it, and approved. Straightway He ordained that the Souls should be incorporated; and they were seized with horror on learning what should be their condemnation.

These words, said Isis, struck me. Hearken, my son Horos, for I teach thee a mystery. Our ancestor Kamephes had it also from Hermes, who inscribes the recital of all things; I, in turn, received it from the ancient Kamephes when he admitted me to the initiation of the black veil; [5] and thou, likewise, O marvellous and illustrious child, receive it from me.

The Souls were about to be imprisoned in bodies, whereat some sighed and lamented, as when some wild and free animal suddenly enchained, in the first moment of subjection to hard servitude and of severance from the beloved habits of the wilderness, struggles and revolts, refusing to follow its conqueror, and if occasion presents itself, slaying him. Others, again, hissed like serpents, or gave vent to piercing cries and sorrowful words, glancing aimlessly from height to depth.

"Great Heaven," said one, "principle of our birth, ether, pure airs, hands, and sacred breath of the sovereign God, and you, shining Stars, eyes of the Gods, unwearying light of Sun and Moon, our early brethren, what grief, what rending is this! Must we quit these vast, effulgent spaces, this sacred sphere, all these splendors of the empyrean and of the happy republic of the Gods, to be precipitated into these vile and miserable abodes? What crime, O wretched ones, have we committed? How can we have merited, poor sinners that we are, the penalties which await us? Behold the sad future in store for us - to minister to the wants of a fluctuating and dissoluble body! No more may our eyes distinguish the souls divine! Hardly through these watery spheres shall we perceive, with sighs, our ancestral heaven; at intervals even we shall cease altogether to behold it. By this disastrous sentence direct vision is denied to us; we can see only by the aid of the outer light; these are but windows that we possess - not eyes. Nor will our pain be less when we hear in the air the fraternal breathing of the winds with which no longer can we mingle our own, since that will have for its dwelling, instead of the sublime and open world, the narrow prison of the breast! But Thou, Who drivest us forth, and causest us from so high a seat to descend so low, assign a limit to our sufferings! O Master and Father, so quickly become indifferent to Thy handiwork, appoint a term to our penance, deign to bestow on us some last words, while yet we are able to behold the expanse of the luminous spheres!"

This prayer of the Souls was granted, my son Horos, for the Lord was present; and sitting upon the throne of Truth, thus He addressed them: -

"O Souls; you shall be governed by Desire and Necessity; after me, these shall be your masters and your guides. Souls, subjected to my sceptre which never fails, know that inasmuch as you remain stainless you shall inhabit the regions of the skies. If among you any be found to merit reproach, they shall inhabit abodes destined to them in mortal organisms. If your faults be light, you shall, delivered from the bond of the flesh, return to heaven. But if you become guilty of graver crime, if you turn away from the end for which you have been formed, then indeed you shall dwell neither in heaven nor in human bodies, but thenceforth you shall pass into those of animals without reason." [6]

Having thus spoken, O my son Horos, He breathed upon them and said, "It is not according to chance that I have ordained your destiny; if you act ill, it will be worse; it will be better if your actions are worthy of your birth. It is myself and not another who will be your witness and your judge. Understand that it is because of your past errors that you are to be punished and shut up in fleshly bodies. In different bodies, as I have already told you, your re-births will be different. Dissolution shall be a benefit, restoring your former happy condition. But if your conduct be unworthy of me, your prudence, becoming blinded and guiding you backwards, will cause you to take for good fortune that which is really a chastisement, and to dread a happier lot as though it were a cruel injury. The most just among you shall, in their future transformations, approximate to the divine, becoming among men, upright kings, true philosophers, leaders and legislators, true seers, collectors of salutary plants, cunning musicians, intelligent astronomers, wise augurs, instructed ministrants: all beautiful and good offices; as among birds are the eagles which pursue not nor devour those of their own kind, and do not permit weaker ones to be attacked in their presence, because justice is in the nature of the eagle; among quadrupeds, the lion, for he is a strong animal, untamed by slumber, in a mortal body performing immortal toils, and by nothing tired nor beguiled; among reptiles, the dragon, because he is powerful, living long, innocent, and a friend of men, allowing himself to be tamed, having no venom, and, leaving old age, approximating to the nature of the Gods; among fishes, the dolphin, for this creature, taking pity on those who fall into the sea, will carry them to land if they still live, and will abstain from devouring them if dead, although it is the most voracious of all aquatic animals."

Having spoken these words, God became an Incorruptible Intelligence (i.e., resumed the unmanifest).

After these things, my son Horos, there arose out of the earth an exceeding powerful Spirit, unencumbered with any corporeal envelope, strong in wisdom, but savage and fearful; although he could not be ignorant of the knowledge he sought, seeing the type of the human body to be beautiful and august of aspect, and perceiving that the souls were about to enter into their envelopes:

"What are these," said he, "O Hermes, Secretary of the Gods?" "These are men," replied Hermes. "It is a rash work," said he, "to make man with such penetrating eyes, such a subtle tongue, such a delicate hearing that can hear even those things which concern him not, such a fine scent, and in. his hands a sense of touch capable of appropriating everything. O generating Spirit, thinkest thou it is well that he should be free from care - this future investigator of the fine mysteries of Nature? Wilt thou leave him exempt from suffering - he whose thought will search out the limits of the earth? Mankind will dig up the roots of plants, they will study the properties of natural juices, they will observe the nature of stones, they will dissect not only animals but themselves, desiring to know how they have been formed. They will stretch forth their daring hands over the sea, and, cutting down the timber of the wild forest, they will pass from shore to shore seeking one another. They will pursue the inmost secrets of Nature even into the heights, and will study the motions of heaven. Nor is this enough; when nothing yet remains to be known than the furthest boundary of the earth, they will seek even there the last extremities of night. If they apprehend no obstacle, if they live exempt from trouble, beyond reach of any fear or of any anxiety, even heaven itself will not arrest their audacity; they will seek to extend their power over the elements. Teach them, then, desire and hope, in such wise that they may know likewise the dread of accident and of difficulty, and the painful sting of expectation deceived. Let the curiosity of their souls have for balance, desire and fear, care and vain hope. Let their souls be a prey to mutual love, to aspirations and varied longings, now satisfied, now deceived, so that even the sweetness of success may be an allurement to draw them towards misfortune. Let the weight of fevers oppress them, and break in them all desire."

Thou sufferest, Horos, in hearing this thy mother's recital? Surprise and wonder seize thee in presence of the evils which now fall upon poor humanity? That which thou art about to hear is still more sad. The speech of Momos pleased Hermes; he deemed his advice good, and he followed it.

"O, Momos," said he, "the nature of the divine breath which enwraps all things shall not be ineffectual! The Master of the universe has charged me to be His agent and overseer. The Deity of the penetrating eye (Adrastia) [7] will observe and direct all events; and for my part, I will design a mysterious instrument, a measure inflexible and inviolable, to which everything shall be subject from birth even to final destruction, and which shall be the bond of created entities. This instrument shall rule that which is on the earth, and all the rest."

It is thus - quoth Hermes - that I spoke to Momos; and forthwith the instrument operated. Straightway the souls were incorporated, and I was praised for my work.

Then the Lord summoned anew the assembly of the Gods. They gathered together, and He thus addressed them:

"Gods, who have received a sovereign and imperishable nature, and the sway of the vast eternity, ye whose office it is to maintain unceasingly the mutual harmony of things, how long shall we govern an empire unknown? How long shall creation re-main invisible to the sun and moon? Let each of us undertake his part in the universe. By the exercise of our power let us put an end to the cohesion of inertia. Let chaos become a fable, incredible to posterity. Inaugurate your great labours; I will direct you."

He said, and immediately the Kosmic unity, until now obscure, was opened, and in the heights appeared the heavens with all their mysteries. The earth, hitherto unstable, grew more solid beneath the brightness of the sun, and stood forth adorned with enfolding riches. All things are beautiful in the eyes of God, even that which to mortals appears uncomely, because all is made according to the divine laws. And God rejoiced in beholding His works filled with movement; and with outstretched hands grasping the treasures of nature. "Take these," He said, "O sacred earth, take these, O venerable one, who art to be the mother of all things, and henceforth let nothing be lacking to thee!"

With these words, opening His divine hands, He poured His treasures into the universal font. But yet they were unknown, for the souls newly embodied and unable to support their opprobrium, sought to enter into rivalry with the celestial Gods, and, proud of their lofty origin, boasting an equal creation with these, revolted. Thus men became their instruments, opposed to one another, and fomenting civil wars. And thus, force oppressing weakness, the strong burnt and massacred the feeble, and quick and dead were thrust forth from the sacred places.

Then the elements resolved to complain before the Lord of the savage condition of mankind. For the evil being already very grievous, the elements hastened to God the Creator, and pleaded in this wise - the fire being suffered to speak first: - [8]

"O Master," he said, "Maker of this new world, Thou whose name, mysterious among the Gods, has hitherto been revered among all men; how long, O Divinity, halt Thou decreed to leave human life without God? Reveal Thyself to the world which calls for Thee, correct its savage existence by the institution of peace. Grant unto life, law, grant unto night oracles; fill all things with happy auguries; let men fear the judgment of the Gods, and no man shall sin any more. Let crimes receive their just punishment, and men will abstain from unrighteousness. They will fear to violate oaths, and madness will have an end. Teach them gratitude for benefits, so shall I devote my flame to pure offerings and libations, and the altars shall yield Thee exhalations of sweet savours. For now I am polluted, O Master, because the impious temerity of men forces me to consume flesh. They will not suffer me to remain in my nature; they pervert and corrupt my purity!"

The air spoke in its turn: - "I am defiled by the effluvium of corpses, O Master; I am becoming pestilent and unwholesome, and from on high I witness things which I ought not to behold."

Then the water took up the word, and spoke on this wise, O my illustrious son: -

"Father and wondrous Creator of all things, Divinity incarnate, Author of Nature who brings forth all through Thee, command the waters of the streams to be always pure, for now both rivers and seas are compelled to bathe the destroyer and to receive his victims!"

Then at the last the earth appeared, O my glorious son, and thus began: -

"O King, Chief of celestial choirs and Lord of their orbits, Master and Father of the elements which lend to all things increase and decrease, and into which all must return; behold how the impious and insensate tribe of man overspreads me, O venerable One, since by Thy commands I am the habitation of all beings, bearing them all and receiving into my bosom all that is slain; such is now my reproach. Thy terrestrial world in which all creatures are contained is bereft of God. And because they revere nothing, they transgress every law and overwhelm me with all manner of evil works.

To my shame, O Lord, I admit into myself the product of the corruption of carcases. But I, who receive all things, would fain also receive God. Grant to earth this grace, and if Thou comest not Thyself - for indeed I cannot contain Thee - let me at least receive some holy efflux of Thee. Let the earth become the most glorious of all the elements; and since she alone gives all things to all, may she revere herself as the recipient of Thy favours."

Thus the elements discoursed, and forthwith God filled the universe with His divine voice. "Go," said He, "sacred offspring, worthy of your Father's greatness, seek not to change anything, nor refuse to my creatures your ministry. I will send you an efflux of myself, a pure Being who shall investigate all actions, who shall be the dreadful and incorruptible Judge of the living; and sovereign justice shall extend its reign even into the shades beneath the earth. Thus shall every man receive his merited deserts."

Thereupon the elements ceased from their complaints, and each of them resumed its functions and its sway.

And in what manner, O my mother, said Horos, did the earth afterwards obtain this efflux of God?

I will not recount this Nativity, said Isis; I dare not, O powerful Horos, declare the origin of thy race, lest men in the future should learn the generation of the Gods. I will say only that the Supreme God, Creator and Architect of the world, at length accorded to earth for a season, thy father Osiris and the great Goddess Isis, that they might bring the expected salvation. By them life attained its fulness; savage and bloody wars were ended; they consecrated temples to the Gods their ancestors, and instituted oblations. They gave to mortals law, nourishment, and raiment. "They shall read," Hermes said, "my mystic writings, and dividing them into two parts, they shall keep certain of them, and inscribe upon columns and obelisks those which may be useful to man." Institutors of the first tribunals, they established everywhere the reign of order and justice. With them began the faith of treaties, and the introduction into human life of the religious duty of oaths. They taught the rites of sepulture towards those who cease to live; they interrogated the horrors of death; they shewed that the spirit from without delights to return into the human body, and that if the way of entry be shut against it, it brings about a failure of life. Instructed by Hermes, they engraved upon hidden tables that the air is filled with genii. Instructed by Hermes in the secret laws of God, they alone were the teachers and legislators of mankind, initiating them in the arts, the sciences, and the benefits of civilised life. Instructed by Hermes concerning the sympathetic affinities which the Creator has established between heaven and earth, they instituted religious representations and sacred mysteries. And, considering the corruptible nature of all bodies, they ordained prophetic initiation, so that the prophet who lifts his hands to the Gods should be instructed in all things, and that thereby philosophy and magic might provide nourishment for the soul, and medicine might heal the sufferings of the flesh.

Having performed all these things, O my son, and seeing the world arrived at its fulness, Osiris and I were recalled by the inhabitants of heaven; but we could not return thither without having first praised the Lord, so that the celestial Vision might fill the expanse, and that the way of a happy ascension might open before us, since God delights in hymns.

O my mother, said Horos, teach me this hymn, that I also may be instructed in it.

Hearken, my son, answered Isis...

Footnotes

1 This sentence is very obscure; the participles are in the masculine, as though the author had forgotten that a goddess was speaking. I believe the text of the passage must have been altered.

2 This recital of the creation of the souls recalls the Timæus of Plato. After all the Gods were born, the Artificer of the universe thus addressed them: "Gods of gods, of whom I am the Creator and Father, and who, formed by me, are by my will indissoluble, learn what I now say to you.... In order that mortal natures may exist, and that the universe may be indeed universal, turn yourselves according to your nature to the formation of animals, imitating the power which I employed in the generation of yourselves.... I myself will deliver the seeds and beginnings; and for the rest do you weave together the mortal and immortal nature, constructing and producing animals." He said, and into the same cup in which He had mingled and tempered the soul of the universe, He poured the residue, and mixed it in the same manner, but in less pure combinations of a second and third order. And having constituted the universe, He allotted souls to the stars in equal number, distributing each to each; and causing every one to mount his vehicle, He displayed to them the nature of the universe, and taught them the laws of Destiny.

[It may be added, also, that this legend, quaint and grotesque as it is in many of its details, is, likewise, in accord with the Kabbala, which recounts the pre-mundane history of the souls, their creation, their transgression, and their punishment, in much the same fashion. The creation of the visible world by the "working gods," or Titans, as agents for the Supreme God, is a thoroughly Hermetic idea, recognizable in all religious systems, and in accord with modern scientific research, which shews us everywhere the Divine Power operating secretly through natural forces.

3 In reading this allegory, it must be borne in mind that the word "Soul" is used as a general term for all Egos or Intelligences, whether Genii or Men. Further, that in these Fragments, as in the Hebrew Scriptures, the same truths are repeated under different symbols in different passages. Hence the creation of Nature and of "differentiated forms" has already been otherwise depicted in a previous paragraph; and the whole process of the evolution of the Soul has been epitomized in the fable of the making of the protoplasm. The descent into generation occurs, actually, when the Titans first begin the manipulation of this protoplasm. The human body, although last in manifestation, is really the first in the Divine intention, and is the ultimate cause of all the series of objective forms. Hermetically speaking, there is nothing in the whole universe, save Man.

4 Heeren sees in these metaphors an allusion to the creation of Pandora in Hesiod. They recall also a passage in the Pymander, wherein the Rulers of the Seven Planets cause Man to participate in their nature; an idea developed likewise by Macrobius in his commentary on the Dream of Scipio. - Lib. L., chap. xii.

5 Canter translates this by atramenturn, which would signify initiation by writing; but it is possible that the heads of the initiated persons were covered with a black veil, or perhaps the veil of Isis is here intended.

6 It has been questioned whether Hermetic doctrine affirms the Hindu theory of transmigration, to wit - the possibility of the passage of the guilty Ego into lower forms than that of man. We must, I hold, admit the orthodoxy of the doctrine, which, when rightly understood, involves no paradox. In the Divine Pymander, it is clearly set forth that if a human soul continue evil "it shall neither taste of immortality nor be partaker of the good, but being drawn back it returneth into creeping things; and this is the condemnation of an evil soul." Yet, Trismegistus hastens immediately to explain and qualify this statement by adding that such a calamity cannot befall any truly human soul - that is, a soul possessing the divine Mind, however fallen from grace, for so long as the soul retains this living fire it is the soul of a man, and man "is not to be compared to any brute beast upon the earth, but to them that are above in heaven, that are called Gods." But there is a condition so low and lost that at length the divine flame is quenched, and the soul is left dark and Godless, a human soul no longer. "And such a soul, O Son," says Hermes, "hath no Mind; wherefore neither must such an one be called Man." Therefore, while it is true that "no other body is capable of a human soul, neither is it lawful for a man's soul to fall into the body of an unreasonable living thing," so also is it true that a soul, bereft of its Divine Particle which alone made it human, is human no longer, and, following the universal law of

affinity, straightway gravitates to its proper level, sinking to its similars, and drawn to its analogues. Nevertheless, when its purgation is accomplished, such a soul may "come to itself and say, I will arise and go unto my Father."

There are some Rabbis indeed who have thought such an occult significance to lie hid in the parable of the prodigal; swine being accounted universally a figure of lust and sordid desire. The Hermetic doctrine, thus interpreted, is identical with that of the Kabbala on the same point, as we shall elsewhere have occasion to shew; and also with the teaching of Apollonius of Tyana. - (v. Perfect Way, III., 21, etc.)

7 This name appears to have been a marginal interpolation, inserted into the text by a copyist. It serves as a key to what follows, Adrastia (or Nemesis) being the personification of the necessary law (or inflexible instrument) of which Hermes is about to speak.

8 In the Book of Enoch a similar legend appears - "The Giants turned themselves upon men to devour them, and began to do evil to birds and beasts of the field and reptiles and fish; and they devoured with one accord their flesh and drank their blood. When the earth lifted up her voice against the unjust, ... and because of the perdition of men, a cry arose that came even unto heaven. Therefore, Michael and Gabriel, and Souryan and Ouryan, looked forth from the height of heaven, and beheld the abundance of blood that was shed upon the earth, and all the iniquity that was accomplished, and they said one to another: - The voice of their cries ascends, the clamour of the earth is heard even at the gates of heaven, and before you, O holy ones of the skies, the souls of men complain, saying - Avenge us in the presence of the Lord. (VII. 14, 15; VIII. 8, 9; IX. 1, 2, 3.)

[See also the first book of Ovid's Metamorphoses, V., VI., VII. In all these accounts it appears that mankind is inspired to wickedness and impiety by the Giants, who are, in Hermetic teaching, explained to be the lower mundane forces, or "fallen Angels." They are, probably, the first created "souls" mentioned in an early passage of the allegory, and are elsewhere spoken of as Demons. Almost all the poets, whether Hebrew, Hellenic, Hindu, Persian, Norse, or Christian, celebrate the revolt of the Giants against heaven. It is needless to remind the reader that all these sacred fables have an esoteric and individual application, related to the Microcosm within man, as well as to the Macrocosm or world without. The text is manifestly imperfect.

A.K.]

PART II.

O my illustrious son, if thou wilt know any-thing further, ask it of me. And Horos said, Revered Mother, I would fain know how royal souls are born. And Isis answered: - Herein, my son Horos, lies the distinctive character of royal souls. There are in the universe, four regions, governed by a fixed and immutable law: heaven, the ether, the air, and the most holy earth. Above, in heaven, dwell the Gods, ruled as are all the rest, by the Maker of the universe; in the ether are the stars, governed by the great fire, the sun; in the air are the souls of the genii, governed by the moon; upon earth are men and other animals governed by the soul who, for the time, is their king. For the Gods themselves engender those who shall be kings befitting the terrestrial race. Princes are the issue of kings, and he who is most kingly, is a greater king than the rest. [1] The sun, nearer to God than is the moon, is greater and stronger than she, and to him she is subject as much by rank as by power. The king is the last of the Gods and the first of men. So long as he sojourns upon earth, his divinity is concealed, but he possesses something which distinguishes him from other men and approximates him to God. The soul in him comes from a loftier region than that from which descend the souls of common men. Souls destined to reign upon the earth descend thither for two causes. There are those who in former lives have lived blameless, and who merit apotheosis; for such as these royalty is a preparation for the divine state. Again, there are holy souls who, for some slight infringement of the interior and divine law, receive in royalty a penance whereby the suffering and shame of incarnation are mitigated. The condition of these in taking a body resembles not that of others; they are as blessed as when they were free. [2]

As to the various characters of these kings, the variety is not in the souls, for all are royal, but it is due to the nature of the angels and genii who assist them. For souls destined to such offices are not without ministers and escort. Heavenly justice, even while exiling them from the abodes of the Blessed, treats them as their nature befits. When, then, O my son Horos, the ministering angels and genii appointed are warlike, the soul in their charge takes that character, forgetting its own, or rather laying it aside until some future change of condition. If the guardian angels are of a gentle order, then the soul follows its path in peace; if they are friends of judgment, the soul loves to judge; if they are musicians, then the soul sings; if they love truth, the soul is that of a philosopher. Thus the souls necessarily follow the teaching of their guardians; falling into human bodies they forego their proper estate, and while exiled from it they approximate to those intelligences by whom they have been embodied.

Thine explanation is complete, my mother, said Horos, but thou hast not yet informed me in what manner noble souls are born.

There are upon earth, O my son, different offices. So also is it among souls; they occupy different stations, and that soul which issues from a more exalted sphere is nobler than the rest; even as he who is free among men, is nobler than the slave. Exalted and royal souls are necessarily the masters of men.

How are souls born male or female?

Souls, my son Horos, are all equal in nature, since they come from one region wherein the Creator has formed them. There are not among them either males or females; this distinction exists only between bodies, and not between incorporeal beings. But some are more energetic, some are gentler; and this belongs to the air in which all things are formed. For an airy body envelopes the soul; in it are the elements of earth, water, air, and fire. Among females this combination contains more of cold and of moisture than of dryness and heat, and the soul which is enfolded therein is watery and disposed to softness. The contrary happens among males; their envelope contains more of dryness and of heat, less of cold and of moisture; hence in bodies so formed the souls manifest greater vivacity and energy.

And how, O my mother, are born the souls of the wise?

And Isis answered: - The organ of vision is enveloped in tunics. When these tunics are thick and dense, the sight is dull; when they are fine and subtle, the sight is penetrating. Even so is it with the soul; she likewise has her coverings, incorporeal as herself. These coverings are the interior airs; when they are subtle, clear, and transparent, then the soul is perspicuous; when, on the contrary, they are dense, thick, and turgid, then she cannot see far; and discerns only, as though in cloudy weather, that which lies immediately before her steps.

And Horos said: - For what reason, my mother, are the minds of men who are not of our holy country less open than the minds of those who belong to it? And Isis replied [3]: - The earth is set in the midst of the universe like a man lying on his back and gazing into heaven, and the various regions of earth correspond to the different members of the man. The earth turns her gaze towards heaven as towards her father, following in her changes the changes of the skies. Her head lies to the south, her right shoulder to the east, her left is turned towards the Lybian wind, her feet are under the constellation of the Bear, the right beneath the tail, and the left beneath the head of the Bear; her loins are under the regions of heaven nearest to the Bear; the midst of her body is beneath the centre of heaven. Behold as a proof of these things, how they who dwell in the South have a beautiful countenance and plentiful hair, while the orientals have hands hardy in conflict and ready with the bow, for they are right-handed; the westerns are strong and fight with the left hand, attributing to the left side the functions which belong in others to the right; those who dwell beneath the Bear are distinguished by the attributes of their feet, and by the beauty of their legs; those who inhabit beyond the Bear in the climate of Italy and of Greece are remarkable for the beauty of their loins, and hence their tendency to prefer males. This part of the body also, being whiter than the rest, produces men of a whiter hue. The hallowed region of our ancestors is in the midst of the earth, and since the midst of the human body is the seat of the heart, and the heart of the soul, this is why, my son, the men of this land, beside the qualities which all men possess in common, have also a loftier intelligence and wisdom, because the heart of the earth brings them forth and nourishes them.

Moreover, my son, the south is the storehouse of the clouds; it is there they assemble, and thence, it is said, flows our river (Nile), when the cold becomes abundant. Now, where the clouds descend, the air grows thick and is filled with vapours which spread themselves as a veil not only over the sight, but over the intelligence. The east, my son Horos, is continually disturbed and glowing under the sunrise, as is the west under the sunset; there-fore, they who dwell in these regions can hardly preserve a clear perception. The north, by means of its icy temperature, thickens the mind even as it does the body. The central land alone, clear and serene, is favoured as are those who inhabit her. She brings forth in a perpetual tranquillity, she adorns and completes her offspring, she contends alone against all others, she triumphs, and like a worthy ruler partakes with the vanquished the fruits of victory.

Explain to me further, my august Mother, what it is that causes in living men during long maladies, an alteration of discernment, of reason, even of the soul itself.

And Isis answered: - Among animals there are those who have affinity with fire, others with water, others with earth, others with air, others again with two or three elements, or with all the four. Or, inversely, some have an antipathy for fire, some for water, some for earth, some for air, or again for two, three or four elements. Thus, the locust and all kinds of insects flee from the fire; the eagle, the hawk, and other birds of flight fear the water; the fish dread the air and earth; the serpent abhors the open air, and like all crawling creatures loves the ground; all fishes delight in the deep, the birds in the air where they pass their lives; those who fly highest delight in the fire (of the sun) and sojourn in its vicinity. There are even certain creatures who disport themselves in the fire, such are the salamanders who have their abode in it. The elements enfold the body, and every soul inhabiting a body is weighed down and enchained by the four elements; wherefore, it is natural that the soul should have affinity with certain elements and aversion for others, for which reason she cannot enjoy perfect happiness. Nevertheless, as the soul is of divine origin, she struggles and meditates even beneath this bodily covering; but her thoughts are not what they would be if she were free from the body. And if the body be disturbed and troubled by sickness or by terror, the soul herself is tossed about like a man in the midst of tempestuous waves.

Footnotes

1 This must not be understood in a vulgar sense of mere earthly monarchy, but of souls whose destiny it is to be chiefs and leaders among men, whether spiritually, intellectually, or politically.

2 This passage perhaps refers, though obscurely, to Avatars of souls who have already attained beatitude, though not apotheosis.

3 I believe the whole of the ensuing passage to be highly metaphorical, and to relate to the occult distinctions and divisions of the seven great races of mankind. It is not difficult to interpret the allusions.

A.K.

PART III.

Thou hast given me admirable instruction, O my most powerful Mother Isis, concerning the marvellous creation of Souls by God, and I am filled with wonder; but thou hast not yet shewn me whither souls depart when set free from bodies. Fain would I contemplate this mystery, and thank only thee for the initiation.

And Isis said: - Hearken, my son, for thy most necessary enquiry holds an important place, and may not be neglected. Hear my reply.

O great and marvellous scion of the illustrious Osiris, think not that souls on quitting the body mix themselves confusedly in the vague immensity and become dispersed in the universal and infinite spirit, without power to return into bodies, to preserve their identity, or to seek again their primeval abode. Water spilt from a vase returns no more to its place therein, it has no proper locality, it mingles itself with the mass of waters; but it is not thus with souls,

O most wise Horos. I am initiated into the mysteries of the immortal nature; I walk in the ways of the truth, and I will reveal all to thee without the least omission. And first I will tell thee that water, being a body without reason, composed of myriads of fluid particles, differs from the soul which is, my son, a personal entity, the royal work of the hands and of the mind of God, abiding herself in intelligence. That which proceeds from Unity, and not from multiplicity, cannot mingle with other things, and in order that the soul may be joined to the body, God subjects this harmonious union to Necessity.

Souls do not, then, return confusedly, nor by chance, into one and the same place, but each is despatched into the condition which belongs to her. And this is deter-mined by that which the soul experiences while yet she is in the tenement of the body, loaded with a burden contrary to her nature. Hear: therefore, this comparison, O beloved Horos; suppose that there should be shut up in the same prison, men, eagles, doves, swans, hawks, swallows, sparrows, flies, serpents, lions, leopards, wolves, dogs, hares, oxen, sheep, and certain amphibious animals, such as seals, hydras, turtles, crocodiles, and that at the same moment all the creatures should be liberated. All at once would escape; the men would seek cities and the public places, the eagles the ether, where nature teaches them to live, the doves the lower air, the hawks the higher expanse; the swallows would repair to places frequented by men, the sparrows to the orchards, the swans to districts where they could sing; the flies would haunt the proximity of the ground as high only as human exhalations extend, for the property of flies is to live on these and to flit over the surface of the earth; the lions and leopards would flee to the mountains, the wolves to the solitudes; the dogs would follow the track of man; the hares would betake themselves to the woods, the oxen to the fields and meadows, the sheep to the pastures; the serpents would seek the caves of the earth; the seals and the turtles would rejoin their kind in the shallows and running waters, in order to enjoy, conformably to their nature, alike the proximity of the shore and of the deep. Each creature would return, conducted by its own interior discernment, into the abode befitting it. Even so every soul, whether human or inhabiting the earth under other conditions, knows whither she ought to go; unless, indeed, some son of Typhon should pretend that a bull may subsist in the waters or a turtle in the air. If, then, even when immersed in flesh and blood, souls do not infringe the law of order, although under penance, - for union with the body is a penance, - how much more shall they conform thereto when delivered from their bonds and set at liberty!

Now this most holy law, which extends even unto heaven, is on this wise, O illustrious child: behold the hierarchy of souls! The expanse between the empyrean and the moon is occupied by the Gods, the stars, and the powers of providence. Between the moon and ourselves, my son, is the abode of the souls. The unmeasured air, which we call the wind, has in itself an appointed way in which it moves to refresh the earth, as I shall by and by relate. But this movement of the air upon itself impedes not the way of the souls, nor does it hinder them from ascending and descending without obstacle; they flow across the air without mingling in it, or confounding themselves therewith, as water flows over oil. This expanse, my son, is divided into four provinces, and into sixty regions. The first province from the earth upwards comprehends four regions, and extends as far as certain summits or promontories, which it is unable to transcend. The second province comprises eight regions in which the motions of the winds arise. Be thou attentive, my son, for thou hearest the ineffable mysteries of the earth, the heavens, and of the sacred fluid which lies between.[1] In the province of the winds fly the birds; above this there is no moving air nor any creature. But the air with all the beings it contains distributes itself into all boundaries within its reach, and into the four quarters of the earth, while the earth cannot lift itself into the mansions of the air. The third province comprehends sixteen regions filled with a pure and subtle element. The fourth contains thirty-two regions, in which the air, wholly subtle and diaphanous, allows itself to be penetrated by the element of fire. Such is the order which, without confusion, reigns from depth to height; - to wit, four general divisions, twelve intervals, sixty regions, and in these dwell the souls, each according to the nature thereof. They are indeed all of one substance, but they constitute a hierarchy; and the further any region is removed from the earth, the loftier is the dignity of the souls which dwell therein.

And now it remains to be explained to thee, O most glorious Horos, what souls they are who abide in each of these regions, and this I shall set forth, beginning by the most exalted.

The expanse which stretches between earth and heaven is divided into regions, my son Horos, according to measure and harmony. To these regions our ancestors have given various names; some call them zones, others firmaments, others spheres. Therein dwell the souls who are freed from bodies, and those who have not yet been incorporated. The stations which they occupy correspond with their dignity. In the upper region are the divine and royal souls; the baser souls - they who float over the surface of the earth - are in the lowest sphere, and in the middle regions are the souls of ordinary degree. Thus, my son, the souls destined to rule descend from the superior zones, and when they are delivered from the body, thither they return, or even higher still, unless indeed they have acted contrary to the dignity of their nature and to the laws of God. For, if they have transgressed, the

Providence on high causes them to descend into the lower regions according to the measure of their faults; and in like manner also it conducts other souls, inferior in power and dignity, from the lower spheres into a more exalted abode. For on high dwell two ministers of the universal Providence; one is guardian of the souls, the other is their conductor, who sends them forth and ordains for them bodies. The first minister guards them, the second releases or binds them, according to the will of God.

In this wise the law of equity presides over the changes which take place above, even as upon earth also it moulds and constructs the vessels in which the souls are immured. This law is supplemented by two energies, Memory and Experience. Memory directs in Nature the preservation and maintenance of all the original types appointed in heaven; the function of Experience is to provide every soul descending into generation with a body appropriate thereto; so that passionate souls should have vigorous bodies; slothful souls sluggard bodies; active souls active bodies; gentle souls gentle bodies; powerful souls powerful bodies; cunning souls dexterous bodies; - briefly, that every soul should have a befitting nature. For it is not without just cause that winged creatures are clothed with feathers; that intelligent creatures are gifted with finer senses and superior to others; that beasts of the field are furnished with horns, with tusks, with claws, or other weapons; that reptiles are endowed with undulating and flexible bodies, and lest the moisture of their natures should render them feeble, are armed either with teeth or with pointed scales, so that they are, even less than others, in peril of death. As for fishes, these timid souls have allotted to them for a dwelling-place that element in which light is bereft of its double activity, for in the water, fire neither illuminates nor burns. Each fish, swimming by the help of his spiny fins, flies where he wills, and his weakness is protected by the obscurity of the deep. Thus are souls immured in bodies resembling themselves; in human shape, those souls who have received reason; in flying creatures, souls of a wild nature; in beasts, souls without reason, whose only law is force; in reptiles, deceitful souls, for they attack not their prey face to face, but by ambush; while fishes enshrine those timid souls who merit not the enjoyment of other elements.

In every order of animals there are individuals who transgress the laws of their being.

In what way, my Mother? said Horos.

And Isis answered: In this wise: - A man who acts against reason, a beast which eludes necessity, a reptile which forgets its cunning, a fish which loses its timidity, a bird which renounces freedom. Thou hast heard what was to be said concerning the hierarchy of souls, their descent, and the creation of bodies.

O my son, in every order of souls there are found a few royal souls, and of divers characters: some fiery, some cold, some proud, some gentle, some crafty, some simple, some contemplative, some active. This diversity belongs to the regions from whence they descend into bodies. From the royal zone the royal souls go forth, but there are many royalties; the royalty of spirit, of the flesh, of art, of science, of the virtues.

And how, said Horos, dost thou name these royalties?

O my son, the king of souls who have hitherto existed is thy father Osiris; the king of bodies is the prince of each nation, he who governs. The king of wisdom is the Father of all things; the Initiator is the thrice great Hermes; over medicine presides Asclepios, the son of Hephaistos; force and power are under the sway of Osiris, and after him, under thine, my son. Philosophy depends on Arnebaskenis; poetry, yet again, on Asclepios, Imouthè's son. So that, if thou thinkest thereon, thou wilt perceive that there are indeed many royalties and many kings.

But the supreme royalty belongs to the highest region; lesser kingships correspond to the spheres which bring them forth. Those who issue from the fiery zone handle fire; those who come from the watery zone frequent liquid spheres; from the region of art and learning those are born who devote themselves to art and science; from the region of inactivity, those who live in ease and idleness. All that is done and said upon earth has its origin in the heights, from whence all essences are dispensed with measure and equilibrium; nor is there anything which does not emanate from above and return thither.

Explain to me this that thou sayest, O my Mother.

And Isis answered: - An evident token of these exchanges has been stamped on all creatures by most holy Nature. The breath which we indraw from the upper air we exhale and again inbreathe by means of the lungs within us which perform this work. And when the way destined to receive our breath is closed, then no longer do we remain on earth; we depart hence. Moreover, O my glorious son, there are other accidents by which the balance of our combination may be destroyed. [2]

What is, then, this combination, O my Mother?

It is the union and admixture of the four elements, whence emanates a vapour which envelops the soul, penetrates into the body and communicates to both its own character. Thus are produced varieties among souls and bodies. If in the composition of a body, fire dominates, then the soul being already of an ardent nature, receives thereby an excess of heat which renders it the more energetic and furious, and the body the more vivacious and active.

If the air dominates, the body and soul of the creature are thereby rendered unstable, errant and restless. The domination of the water causes the soul to be mild, affable, bland, sociable, and easily moulded, because water blends and mixes itself readily with all other things, dissolves them if it be abundant, moistens and penetrates them if it be less in quantity. A body softened by too much humidity offers but a weak resistance, a slight malady disintegrates it, and little by little dissolves its cohesion. Again, if the earthy element be dominant, the soul is obtuse, because the body lacks subtlety, nor can she force a way through the density of its organism. Therefore, the soul remains indrawn upon herself, borne down by the burden she supports, and the body is solid, inactive, and heavy, moving only with effort.

But if the elements be all in just equilibrium, then the whole nature is ardent in its actions, subtle in its motions, fluent in its sensations, and of a robust constitution. Of the predominance of air and fire birds are born, whose nature resembles that of the elements which generate them. Men are endowed with an abundance of fire united with but a little air, and of water and earth equal parts. This excess of fire becomes sagacity, seeing that intelligence is indeed a kind of flame, which consumes not, but which penetrates. The predominance of water and earth with a sufficient admixture of air and but little fire engenders beasts; those endued with more fire than the rest are the more courageous. Water and earth in equal quantities give birth to reptiles, which, being deprived of fire, have neither courage nor truthfulness, while the excess of water renders them cold, that of earth, sordid and heavy, and the lack of air makes all their movements difficult. Much water with but little earth produces fishes; the absence of fire and air in them causes their timidity, and disposes them to lie hidden, while the predominance of water and earth in their nature approximates them by natural affinity to earth dissolved in water. Moreover, by means of the proportional increase of the elements composing the body is the body itself increased, and its development ceases when the full measure is attained. And so long, my beloved son, as equilibrium is maintained in the primitive combination and in the vapours arising therefrom, that is, so long as the normal proportion of fire, air, earth, and water remains unchanged, the creature continues in health. But if the elements deviate from the proportion originally determined - (I speak not now of the growth of activities, nor of that resulting from a change of order, but of a rupture of equilibrium whether by addition or diminution of fire or of other elements) - then malady supervenes. And should air and fire, whose nature is one with that of the soul itself, prevail in the conflict, then, through the dominance of those elements, destroyers of the flesh, the creature abandons its proper state. For the earthy element is the pabulum of the body, and the water wherewith it is permeated contributes to consolidate it; but it is the aerial element which confers motion, and the fire engenders all energies. The vapours produced by the union and combination of these elements blending with the soul, as it were by fusion, bear her along with them, and clothe her in their own nature, whether good or evil. So long as she remains in this natural association the soul keeps the rank she has attained. But if a change should occur either in the combination itself or in any of its parts or subdivisions, the vapours, altering their condition, alter likewise the relations between soul and body; the fire and air, aspiring upward, draw with them the soul, their sister, while the watery and terrestrial elements, which tend earthwards like the body, weigh it down and overwhelm it.

Footnotes

1 This hint is enough to indicate that Isis speaks in metaphorical language. The entire description should be understood as equally applicable to the macrocosm and the microcosm, the consciousness of every constituent particle in man's system being accounted a soul.
2 Isis here speaks not as a Goddess, but as a mortal.

A.K.

END OF THE VIRGIN OF THE WORLD

BOOK II

A TREATISE ON INITIATIONS; OR, ASCLEPIOS

PART I

Hermes:

It is a God who hath brought thee to us, Asclepios, that thou mayst assist at a divine discourse, and one which will be the most truly religious of all we have as yet held, or with which we have been inspired from on high. In understanding it thou wilt be in possession of all blessings, - if so be indeed there are several, and if it be not more correct to say there is but one blessing which comprises all. For each one of them is bound to another; all are derived from one and make but one, so that their mutual bonds make separation impossible. This is what thou wilt understand by paying attention to that which we are about to say. But first, Asclepios, go away for a little while and look for another hearer for our discourse.

[Asclepios proposes to call Ammon.]

There is no objection to Ammon's presence among us, says Trismegistos. I have not forgotten that I have addressed to him, as to a dear son, several writings on Nature and other subjects relating to exoteric teaching. But it is thy name, Asclepios, which I shall inscribe at the head of the present treatise. And call no other person than Ammon. For a discourse upon the holiest matters of religion would be profaned by a too numerous audience. It is an impiety to deliver to the knowledge of a great number, a treatise full of divine majesty. [1]

[Ammon enters the sanctuary, and completes the holy quartet, [2] filled with the presence of God. The invitation to devotional silence comes from the lips of Hermes, and in the presence of the attentive souls who hang upon his words, the divine Love thus begins: -] [3]

Every human soul, Asclepios, is immortal; but this immortality is not uniform. It differs both in mode and in duration.

Asclepios:

It is because souls, Trismegistos, are not all of the same quality.

Hermes:

How quickly thou understandest the reason of things, Asclepios! I have not yet said that all is one and that one is all, since all things were in the Creator before the creation and we can call Him all since all things are His members. Wherefore, throughout all this discourse, bear in mind Him who is One and All, the Creator of all things.

Everything descends from heaven upon the earth, into the water, into the air: only fire is vivifying, because it tends upwards; that which tends downwards is subordinate to it. That which descends from above is generative; that which emanates and rises is nutritive. The earth, alone self-supported, is the receptacle of all things, and reconstructs the types which she receives. That Universal Being which contains all and which is all, puts into motion the soul and the world, all that nature comprises. In the manifold unity of universal life, the innumerable individualities distinguished by their variations, are, nevertheless, united in such a manner that the whole is one, and that everything proceeds from unity.

Now this unity, which constitutes the world, is formed of four elements: fire, water, earth, and air: - one single world, one single soul, and one single God. Lend me now all the powers and all the penetration of thy thought; for the idea of Divinity, which cannot be conceived save by divine assistance, resembles a rapid stream precipitating itself onwards with impetuosity, and often, therefore, outstrips the attention of the listeners, and even of him who teaches.

Footnotes

1 It is the indiscriminate disclosure of spiritual mysteries to those who, by reason of their exclusively fleshly condition, are incapable of appreciating and reverencing then, that is called by Jesus a casting of pearls before swine.

2 The fourth being Tatios, the son of Trismegistos. All such discourses required - for occult reasons - the presence of a minimum number of four. The four above represented the four great divisions of existence, and constituted an epitome of the Universe. "The form of the fourth is like the Son of God," Nabuchodonosor is made to exclaim in the Hermetic allegory in Daniel, representing the transmutation - instead of the expected destruction - of the earthly elements of Man under the fiery alchemic ordeal of suffering.

3 This identification of Hermes with Eros - the only instance Dr. Menard says he has found in literature - accords with the Hermetic axiom - " Love and Wisdom are One."

A.K.

PART II

Heaven - God manifest - regulates all bodies. Their growth and their decline are determined by the sun and the moon. But He who directs heaven - the soul itself and all that exists in the world - is very God, the Creator.

From the heights where He reigns descend innumerable influences which spread themselves throughout the world, into all souls both general and particular, and into the nature of things.

The world has been prepared by God in order to receive all particular forms. Realising these forms by means of Nature, He has updrawn the world to heaven through the four elements.

Everything is in accordance with the designs of God; but that which originates from on high has been separated into individualities in the following manner. The types of all things follow their (representative) individualities in such way that the type is a whole; the individual is a part of the type.

Thus the Gods constitute a type, the genii also. Similarly, men, birds, and all beings which the world contains, constitute types producing individuals resembling them.

There is yet another type, without sensation, but not without soul. It consists of those beings which sustain themselves by means of roots fixed in the earth. Individualities of this type are found everywhere.

Heaven is full of God. The types of which we have spoken have their habitation extending up to that of the beings whose individualities are immortal. For the individuality is a part of the type, as, for instance, man is a part of humanity; and each one follows the character of its type. Hence it comes that, while all types are imperishable, individuals are not all imperishable.

Divinity forms a type of which all the individualisations are as immortal as itself. Among other beings eternity belongs only to the type; the individual perishes, and is perpetuated only by reproduction. There are, then, some mortal individualities. Thus man is mortal, humanity is immortal.

Nevertheless, individuals of all the types mix with all the types. Some are primitive; others are produced by these, by God, by genii, by men, and all resemble their respective types.

For bodies can be formed only by the divine will; individualities cannot be characterised without the aid of the genii; the education and training of animals cannot be conducted without man.

All those genii who have forsaken their own type, and become joined in individuality to an individuality of the divine type, are regarded as neighbours and associates of the Gods.

The genii who preserve the character of their type, and are properly called genii, love that which relates to mankind. The human type resembles, or even surpasses, theirs; for the individuality of the human is manifold and various, and results from the association mentioned above. It is the indispensable link between nearly all other individualities.

The man who has affinity with the Gods through the intelligence which he shares with them, and through piety, is the neighbour of God. He who has affinity with the genii approximates himself to them. They who are satisfied with human mediocrity remain a part of the human type. Other human individualities will be neighbours of the types or individualities with which they shall be in affinity.

PART III

Man, then, Asclepios, is a great marvel; a creature worthy of respect and adoration. For amid this divine Nature he moves as if he himself were a God. He knows the order of the genii, and, aware that he is of the same origin, he despises the human side of his being in order to attach himself exclusively to the divine element.

How happily constituted and near to the Gods is humanity! In joining himself to the divine, man disdains that which he has in him of the earthly; he connects himself by a bond of love to all other beings, and thereby feels himself necessary to the universal order. He contemplates heaven; and in this happy middle sphere in which he is placed, he loves all that is below him, he is beloved of all that is above. He cultivates the earth; he borrows the speed of the elements; his piercing thought fathoms the deeps of the sea. Everything is clear for him. Heaven does not seem to him too high, for knowledge lifts him to it. The brightness of his mind is not obscured by the thick mists of the air; the earth's gravitation is no obstacle to his efforts; the profundity of deep seas does not disturb him; he includes everything and remains everywhere the same.

All animate beings have as it were roots passing downwards; inanimate beings, on the contrary, have a single root passing from below upwards, and supporting a whole forest of branches. Some creatures nourish themselves upon two elements, others upon one only. There are two kinds of aliment for the two portions of the creature - one for the soul and another for the body. The soul of the world sustains itself by perpetual motion. Bodies develop themselves by means of water and of earth, the aliments of the inferior world. The spirit which fills everything, mingles with everything, and vivifies everything, adds consciousness to the intelligence, which, by a peculiar privilege, man borrows from the fifth element - the ether. In man, the consciousness is raised to the knowledge of the divine order.

Since I am led to speak of the consciousness, I will presently expound to you its function, which is great and holy as that of divinity itself. But let us first complete the exposition already begun. I was speaking of union with the Gods - a privilege which they accord only to humanity. A few men only have the happiness of rising to that perception of the Divine which subsists only in God and in the human intelligence.

Asclepios:

Are, then, not all men similarly conscient, Trismegistos?

Hermes:

All, Asclepios, have not the true intelligence. They are deceived when they suffer themselves to be drawn after the image of things, without seeking for the true reason of them. It is thus that evil is produced in man; and that the first of all creatures lowers himself almost to the level of the brutes.

But I will speak to you of the consciousness and all that belongs to it, when I come to my exposition of the mind. For man alone is a dual creature. One of the two parts of which he consists is single, and, as the Greeks say, essential; that is, formed after the divine likeness. The part which the Greeks call Kosmic - that is, belonging to the world - is quadruple, and constitutes the body, which, in man, serves as an envelope to the divine principle. This divine principle, and that which belongs to it, the perceptions of the pure intelligence, conceal themselves behind the rampart of the body. [1]

Footnotes

1 "The five elements of the Microcosm are here made to correspond with the five elements which the Greeks allotted to the Macrocosm; earth, water, air, fire, and ether. Trismegistos says that man obtains his intelligence from "the ether - the fifth element." Trismegistos includes in the body the physical particles, the exterior consciousness, the magnetic forces, and the sensible or mundane mind. In the fifth element he includes the immortal part - soul and spirit; since he speaks of the "divine principle and that which belongs to it - the perceptions of the pure intelligence." The soul, as we have already seen in the "Virgin of the world," is the percipient principle of man; the spirit is the divine light by means of which she sees. It is advisable, in this place, to point out, for the sake of a clear under-standing of what follows, that Hermetic doctrine regards man as having a twofold nature. For he is in one sense a

child of the earth, developed by progressive evolution from below upwards; a true animal, and therefore bound by strict ties of kinship with the lower races, and of allegiance to Nature. In the other sense, man descends from above, and is of celestial origin; because when a certain point in his development from below is reached, the human soul focuses and fixes the Divine Spirit, which is peculiarly the attribute of man, and the possession of which constitutes his sovereignty over all other creatures. And until this vivification of the soul occurs, man is not truly Man in the Hermetic sense.

A.K.

PART IV

Asclepios:
Why then, O Trismegistos, was it necessary that man should be placed in the world, instead of where God is, to dwell with Him in supreme beatitude?
Hermes:
Thy question is natural, O Asclepios, and I pray God to assist me in replying to it, for everything depends upon His will, especially those great things which are at this moment the subject of our enquiry; listen, then, to me, Asclepios. The Lord and Author of all things, whom we call God, brought forth a second God, visible and sensible; I describe him thus, not because he himself has sensibility, for this is not the place to treat such a question, but because he is perceptible to the senses. Having then produced this unique Being who holds the first rank among creatures and the second after Himself, He found His offspring beautiful and filled with all manner of good, and He loved it as His own child.[1] He willed, then, that another should be able to contemplate this Being so great and so perfect whom He had drawn forth from Himself, and to this end He created man, endowed with reason and intelligence.

The will of God is absolute accomplishment; to will and to do are for Him the work of the selfsame instant. And, knowing that the essential could not apprehend all things unless enveloped by the world, He gave to man a body for a dwelling-place. He willed that man should have two natures; He united them intimately and blended them in just proportion.

Thus, He formed man of spirit and of body; of an eternal nature and of a mortal nature, so that, a creature thus constituted, he might, by means of his double origin, admire and adore that which is celestial and eternal; cultivate and govern that which is upon the earth. I speak here of mortal things, not of the two elements subjected to man, to wit, earth and water, but of things coming from man, which are in him or depending on him, such as the culture of the soil, the pastures, the construction of buildings, of ports, navigation, commerce, and those reciprocal exchanges which are the strongest bond among men. Earth and water form a part of the world, and this terrestrial part is sustained by the arts and sciences, without which the world would be imperfect in the eyes of God. For that which God wills is necessary, and the effect accompanies His will; nor can it be believed that anything which has seemed good to Him can cease to seem good to Him, because from the beginning He knew what should be and what should please Him.

Footnotes

1 This "second God" is the Visible Universe, which in most Hermetic writings is spoken of as the "Son of God" - "the word made flesh."

PART V

But I perceive, O Asclepios, that thou art anxious to know in what manner Heaven and those who inhabit it can be the object of the aspiration and adoration of man; learn, then, O Asclepios, that to aspire after the God of heaven and all those who are therein is to render them frequent homage; for alone of all animated beings, divine and human, man is able to render it. The admiration, adoration, praise, and homage of man rejoice heaven and the celestial inhabitants; and the choir of the Muses has been sent among men by the supreme Divinity in order that the terrestrial world might not be without the sweet science of hymns; or rather that the human voice might celebrate Him who only is All, since He is the Father of all things, and that the tender harmonies of earth might ever unite themselves with the celestial choirs. Only a few men, rarely endowed with a pure intelligence, are entrusted with this holy function of beholding heaven clearly. Those in whom the confusion of their two natures holds the intelligence captive under the weight of the body, are appointed to have communion with the inferior elements. Man is not, then, debased because he has a mortal part; on the contrary, this mortality augments his aptitudes and his power; his double functions are possible to him only by his double nature; he is constituted in such a manner that he can embrace alike the terrestrial and the divine. I desire, O Asclepios, that thou mayest bring to this exposition all the attention and all the ardour of thy mind; for many are wanting in faith concerning these things. And now I am about to unfold true principles for the instruction of the holiest intelligences.

PART VI

The Master of Eternity is the first God, the world is the second, man is the third. God, Creator of the world and of all that it contains, governs all this universe and subjects it to the rule of man. And man makes of it the object of his special activity. So that the world and man become the appendage one of the other, and it is with reason that in Greek the world is called Kosmos. Man knows himself and knows the world; he should, therefore, distinguish that which is in accord with himself, that which is for his use and that which has a right to his worship. While addressing to God his praises and his acts of grace, he should venerate the world which is the image of God; remembering that he is himself the second image of God. For God has two similitudes: the world and man. The nature of man being complex, that part of him which is composed of soul, of consciousness, of mind, and of reason is divine, and from the superior elements seems able to mount to heaven; while his cosmic and mundane part, formed of fire, water, earth, and air, is mortal and remains upon the earth; so that what is borrowed from the world may be restored to it.

It is thus that mankind is composed of a divine part and of a mortal part, to wit, the body. The law of this dual being, man, is religion, whose effect is goodness. Perfection is attained when the virtue of man preserves him from desire, and causes him to despise all that is foreign to himself. For terrestrial things, of which the body desires the possession, are foreign to all parts of the divine Thought. Such things may indeed be called possessions, for they are not born with us, they are acquired later. They are then foreign to man, and even the body itself is foreign to man, in such wise that man ought to disdain both the object of desire, and that whereby he is made accessible to desire.

It is the duty of man to direct his soul by reason, so that- the contemplation of the divine may lead him to take but small account of that mortal part which has been joined to him for the sake of the preservation of the lower world. In order that man should be complete in both his parts, observe that each of these possesses four binary subdivisions - to wit, the two hands and the two feet, which, with the other organs of the body, place him in relation with the inferior and terrestrial world. And, on the other hand, he possesses four faculties: sensibility, soul, memory, and foresight, which permit him to know and perceive divine things. He is able, therefore, to include in his investigations, differences, qualities, effects, and quantities. But if he be too much hindered by the weight of the body, he will be unable to penetrate into the true reason of things.

When man, thus formed and constituted, having received for his function from the supreme God, the government of the world and the worship of Divinity, acquits himself well of this double duty, and obeys the holy Will, what should be his recompense? For, if the world is the work of God, he who by his care sustains and augments its beauty, is the auxiliary of the divine Will, employing his body and his daily labour in the service of the work produced by the hands of God. What should be his recompense, if not that which our ancestors have obtained? May it please divine goodness to accord this recompense also to us; all our aspirations and all our prayers tend towards its attainment; may we, delivered from the prison of the body, and from our mortal bonds, return, sanctified and pure, to the divine heritage of our nature!

Asclepios:

What thou sayest is just and true, O Trismegistos! Such indeed is the price of piety towards God, and of care bestowed on the maintenance of the world. But return to the heavens is denied to those who have lived impiously; upon them is imposed a penance which holy souls escape, to wit, migration into other bodies. The end of this discourse, O Trismegistos, brings us to the hope of an eternal future for the soul, as the result of her life in the world. But this future is for some difficult to believe; for others it is a fable; for others, again, perhaps a subject of derision. For it is a sweet thing to enjoy what one possesses in the corporeal life. Therein lies the evil, which, as one may say, turns the soul's head, attaches her to her mortal part, hinders her from knowing her divine part, and is envious of immortality. For I say unto thee, by a prophetic inspiration, no man after us will choose the simple way of philosophy, which lies wholly in application to the study of divine things, and in holy religion. The majority of men obscure philosophy with diverse questions. How come they to encumber it with sciences which ought not to be comprehended in it, or after what manner do they mingle in it diverse questions?

Hermes:

O Asclepios, they mingle in it, by means of subtleties, a diversity of sciences which belong not to it - arithmetic, music, geometry. But pure, philosophy, whose proper object is holy religion, ought to occupy itself with other sciences only in so far as to admire the regular phases of the stars, their positions and their courses, determined by calculation; the dimensions of the earth, its qualities and quantities; the depth of the sea; the power of fire; and to know the effects of all these things, and Nature; to adore Art, the artist, and his divine intelligence. As for music, that is apprehended when one apprehends reason and the divine order of things. For this order by which everything is ranged singly in the unity of the whole, is indeed an admirable harmony and a divine melody.

Asclepios:

What then, after us, will men become?

Hermes:

Misled by the subtleties of the sophists, they will turn aside from the true, pure and holy philosophy. To adore God in the simplicity of thought and of the soul, to venerate His works, to bless His will, which alone is the fulness of good - this is the only philosophy which is not profaned by the idle curiosity of the mind. But enough on this matter.

PART VII

Let us begin to speak of Mind and of other similar things. In the beginning were God and Hylè - it is thus that the Greeks term the first matter or substance of the universe. The Spirit was with the universe, but not in the same manner as with God. The things which constitute the universe are not God, therefore before their birth they were not in existence, but they were already contained in that from which they were produced. For besides and without created things is not only that which is not yet born, but that also which has no generative fecundity, and which can bring forth nothing. Everything which has the power of generating contains in germ all that can be born of it, for it is easy to that which is brought forth to bear that which shall bring forth. But the eternal God cannot and never could be born; He is, He has been, He will be always. The nature of God is to be His own Principle. But matter, or the nature of the world, and mind, although appearing to be brought forth from the beginning, possess the power of birth and of procreation - fecundative energy. For the beginning is in the quality of Nature, who possesses in herself the potentiality of conception and of production. She is then, without any foreign intervention, the principle of creation. It is otherwise with that which possesses only the power of conception by means of mixing with a second nature. The matrix of the universe and of all that it contains appears not to have been itself born, holding however, within it, potentially, all Nature. I call that the matrix which contains all things, for they could not have been without a vehicle to contain them. Everything which exists must exist in some place (or vehicle), neither qualities nor quantities, nor positions, nor effects could be distinguished in things having no place and being nowhere. Thus the world, although not having been born, has in it the principle of all birth; since it affords all things a fitting matrix for conception. It is, then, the sum-total of qualities and of matter susceptible of creation, although not yet created.

Matter, being fecund in all attributes, is able also to engender evil. I put aside, therefore, O Asclepios and Ammon, the question asked by many: - "Could not God hinder evil in the nature of things?" There is absolutely nothing to say to them; but for you I will pursue the discourse begun, and I will give the explanation. They affirm that God ought to have preserved the world from evil; now, evil is in the world as an integral part of it. The sovereign God indeed provided against it inasmuch as was reasonable and possible, when He bestowed upon humanity sentiment, knowledge, and intelligence. By these faculties solely, which place us above other animals, we may escape the snares of evil and vice. The man who is wise and protected by divine intelligence, knows how to preserve himself from such immediately he beholds them, and before he has been entrapped thereby. The foundation of knowledge is supreme goodness. Spirit governs and gives life to all that is in the world; it is an instrument employed by the will of the sovereign God. Thus we ought to comprehend, by intelligence alone, the supreme Intelligible called God. By Him is directed that secondary sensible God (the universe), who contains all spaces, all substances, the matter of all that engenders and produces, - in a word, all that is.

As for the spirit (or Mind), it moves and governs all individual beings in the world according to the nature which God has assigned to them. Matter - Hylè, or the Kosmos - is the receptacle, the motion, the replication of everything which God directs, dispensing to each of them that which is necessary to it, and filling them with spirit according to their qualities.

The form of the universe is that of a hollow sphere, having in itself the cause of its quality or of its figure, wholly invisible; if, choosing any given point of its surface, one should seek to behold its depths, one would be unable to see anything. It appears visible only by means of those special forms whose images appear graven upon it, it shows itself only in effigy; but in reality it is always invisible in itself. Therefore, the centre, the depths of this sphere - if indeed one may call it a place - is in Greek named Hades, the invisible, from eidein, to see, because the centre of a sphere, cannot be seen from without. Moreover, the types or formative appearances were called Ideas, because they are the forms of the Invisible. This interior of the sphere which the Greeks call Hades, because it is invisible, the Latins name Hell (Inferno), on account of its profound position. These are the primordial principles, the first sources, of all things. Everything is in them, or by them, or comes forth from them.

Asclepios:

These principles are, then, O Trismegistos, the universal substance of all individual appearances?

Hermes:

The world nourishes bodies, the spirit nourishes souls. Thought, the heavenly gift which is the happy privilege of humanity, nourishes intelligence, but few men only have an intelligence capable of receiving such a benefit. Thought is a light which illuminates the intelligence, as the sun illuminates the world. And even more, for the light of the sun may be intercepted by the moon, or by the earth when night comes; but when thought has once penetrated into the human soul, it mingles intimately with her nature, and the intelligence can never again be obscured by any cloud. Therefore, with reason, it has been said that the souls of the Gods are intelligences. As for me, I say not this of all of them, but of the great supernal Gods.

PART VIII

Asclepios:
What, O Trismegistos, are the primordial principles of things?
Hermes:
I reveal to thee great and divine mysteries, and in beginning this initiation I implore the favour of heaven. There are many orders of the Gods; and in all there is an intelligible part. It is not to be supposed that they do not come within the range of our senses; on the contrary, we perceive them, better even than those which are called visible, as this discussion will inform thee.

Thou wilt apprehend this fact if thou lendest all thine attention to our discourse; for this order of ideas, so sublime, so divine, so elevated above the intelligence of man, demands an uninterrupted attention without which speech merely flits across the mind and flees away, or rather, returns to its source and is lost therein.

There are, then, Gods superior to all appearances; after them come the Gods whose principle is spiritual; these Gods being sensible, in conformity with their double origin, manifest all things by a sensible nature, each of them illuminating his works one by another.[1] The supreme Being of heaven, or of all that is comprehended under this name, is Zeus, for it is by heaven that Zeus gives life to all things. The supreme Being of the sun is light, for it is by the disk of the sun that we receive the benefit of the light. The thirty-six horoscopes of the fixed stars have for supreme Being or prince, him whose name is Pantomorphos, or having all forms, because he gives divine forms to divers types. The seven planets, or wandering spheres, have for supreme Spirits Fortune and Destiny, who uphold the eternal stability of the laws of Nature throughout incessant transformation and perpetual agitation. The ether is the instrument or medium by which all is produced.

Thus, from the centre to the uttermost parts, everything moves, and relations are established according to natural analogies. That which is mortal approximates to that which is mortal, that which is sensible to that which is sensible. The supreme direction belongs to the supreme Master, in such wise that diversity is resolved into unity. For all things depend from unity or develop from it, and because they appear distant from one another it is believed that they are many, whereas, in their collectivity they form but one, or rather two, Principles. These two Principles, whence all things proceed, and by which all exist, are the substance of which things are formed, and the Will of Him who differentiates them.

Asclepios:

What is the reason of this, O Trismegistos?

Hermes:

It is this, Asclepios. God is the Father, the universal Ruler - or whatever other name yet more holy and religious may be given to Him - and which, because of our intelligence, ought to be held sacred between us; but, in considering His divinity, we cannot define Him by any such name. For the voice is a sound resulting from the concussion of the air, and declaring the will of man, or the impression that his mind has received through the senses. This name, composed of a determined number of syllables, serving as a token between the voice and the ear, and, moreover, sensation, breath, air, all that is concerned with, and belonging to its expression - these convey this name of God, and I do not think that a name, however complex it may be, is able to designate the Principle of all majesty, the Father and Lord of all things. Nevertheless, it is necessary to give Him a name, or rather every name, since He is one and all; therefore we must say either that All is His name, or we must call Him by the names of all things. He, then, who is one and all, possessing the full and entire fecundity of both sexes, ever impregnated by His own Will, brings forth all that He has willed to beget. His Will is universal goodness, the selfsame goodness that exists in all things. Nature is born of His divinity, in such wise that all things should be as they are, and as they have been, and that Nature may suffice to generate of herself all that in the future is to be born. This, O Asclepios, is why and how all things are of two sexes.

Asclepios:

Sayest thou this also of God, O Trismegistos?

Hermes:

Not only of God, but of all beings, whether animated or inanimate. For it is impossible that anything which exists should be barren. Were we to suppress the fecundity of existing things, it would be impossible for them to remain what they are. For I say that this law of generation is contained in Nature, in intellect, in the universe, and preserves all that is brought forth. The two sexes are full of procreation, and their union, or rather their incomprehensible at-one-ment, may be known as Eros, or as Aphrodite, or by both names at once. If the mind can perceive any one truth more certainly and clearly than another, it is this duty of procreation, which God of universal Nature has imposed for ever upon all beings, and to which He has attached the supremest charity, joy, delight, longing, and divinest love. It would be needful to demonstrate the power and necessity of this law, if everyone were not able to recognise and perceive it by interior sentiment. Behold, indeed, how at the moment when from the brain the tide of life descends, the two natures lose themselves each in each, and one eagerly seizes and hides within itself the seed of the other! At this moment, by means of this mutual enchainment, the feminine nature receives the virtue of the male, and the male reposes on the bosom of its mate. This mystery, so sweet and so necessary, is enacted in secret, lest the divinity of the two natures should be constrained to blush before the railleries of the ignorant, were the union of the sexes exposed to irreligious observation. For pious men are not numerous in the world; they are, even, rare, and one might easily count them. In the majority of men malice abides, for lack of prudence and of knowledge of things of the universe.

The understanding of divine religion, the basis of all things, leads to the contempt of all vices in the world, and supplies the remedy against them; but when ignorance asserts itself, then vices develope and inflict upon the soul an incurable hurt. Infected by vices, the soul is, as it were, swollen with poison, and can be healed only by knowledge and understanding. Let us then continue this teaching, even though but a small number should profit by it; and learn thou, O Asclepios, why to man only God has given a part of His intelligence and of His knowledge. Wherefore, hearken.

God the Father and the Ruler, after the Gods,[2] formed men by the union in equal proportions of the corruptible part of the universe and of its divine part, and thus it happened that the imperfections of the universe remained mingled in the flesh. The need of nourishment which we have in common with all creatures, subjects us to desire and to all other vices of the soul. The Gods, constituted of the purest part of Nature, have no need of the aid of reasoning or of study; immortality and eternal youth are for them wisdom and knowledge. Nevertheless, seeing the unity of Order, and that they might not be strangers to these things, God bestowed on them for their reason and their intelligence, the eternal law of Necessity.

Alone, among all creatures, whether to avoid or to overcome the evils of the flesh, man has the aid of reason and of intelligence, and the hope of immortality. Man, created good, and capable of immortal life, has been formed of two natures: one divine, the other mortal; and in thus forming him, the Divine Will rendered him superior to the Gods, who have an immortal nature only, as well as to all mortal beings. For this reason, man, united in close affinity with the Gods, pays them religious service, and the Gods, in their turn, watch with a tender affection over human affairs. But I speak here only of pious men; as for the wicked, I will say nothing concerning them, in order that I may not, by pausing to talk about them, sully the holiness of this discourse.

Footnotes

1 Hermes here includes as Gods the sensible Forces of Nature, the elements and phenomena of the universe.
2 Hermes here intends the mundane deities.
A.K.

PART IX

And since we are brought to speak of the relationship and of the resemblance between men and Gods, behold, O Asclepios, the power and capacity of man! Even as the Ruler and Father, or to give Him the loftiest name - God is the creator of the firmamental Gods, so is man the creator of the Gods who dwell in temples, pleased with human proximity, and not only themselves illumined, but illuminating. And this both profits man and strengthens the Gods. Dost thou marvel, Asclepios? Dost thou lack faith as do many?

Asclepios:

I am confounded, O Trismegistos; but yielding myself willingly to thy words, I judge man to be happy in that he has obtained such felicity.

Hermes:

Certes, he deserves admiration, being the greatest of all the Gods! For the race of the Gods is formed of the purest part of Nature, without admixture of other elements, and their visible signs are, as it were, only heads.[1] But the Gods which mankind makes, possess two natures - one divine, which is the first and by far the purest, the other belonging to humanity, which is the matter of which these Gods are composed, so that they have not only heads, but entire bodies, with all their limbs. Thus mankind, remembering its nature and its origin, persists in this matter, in the imitation of Deity, for even as the Father and Lord has made the eternal Gods after the similitude of Himself, so also has humanity made its Gods in its own image.

Asclepios:

Dost thou speak of the statues, Trismegistos?

Hermes:

Yes, of the statues, Asclepios. See how wanting thou art in faith! Of what else should I speak but of the statues, so full of life, of feeling, and of aspiration, which do so many wonderful things; the prophetic statues which predict the future by bestowing dreams and by all manner of other ways; which strike us with maladies, or heal our pains according to our deserts? Art thou not aware, O Asclepios, that Egypt is the image of heaven, or rather, that it is the projection below of the order of things above? If the truth must be told, this land is indeed the temple of the world. Nevertheless - since sages ought to foresee all things - there is one thing thou must know; a time will come when it will seem that the Egyptians have adored the Gods so piously in vain, and that all their holy invocations have been barren and unheeded. Divinity will quit the earth and return to heaven, forsaking Egypt, its ancient abode, and leaving the land widowed of religion and bereft of the presence of the Gods. Strangers will fill the earth, and not only will sacred things be neglected, but - more dreadful still - religion, piety, and the adoration of the Gods will be forbidden and punished by the laws. Then, this earth, hallowed by so many shrines and temples, will be filled with sepulchres and with the dead. O Egypt! Egypt! there will remain of thy religions only vague legends which posterity will refuse to believe; only words graven upon stones will witness to thy devotion! The Scythian, the Indian, or some other neighbouring barbarian will possess Egypt! Divinity will return to heaven; humanity, thus abandoned, will wholly perish, and Egypt will be left deserted, forsaken of men and of Gods!

To thee I cry, O most sacred River, to thee I announce the coming doom! waves of blood, polluting thy divine waters, shall overflow thy banks; the number of the dead shall surpass that of the living; and if, indeed, a few inhabitants of the land remain, Egyptians by speech, they will in manners be aliens! Thou weepest, O Asclepios! But yet sadder things than these will come to pass. Egypt will fall into apostacy, the worst of all evils. Egypt, once the holy land beloved of the Gods and full of devotion for their worship, will become the instrument of perversion, the school of impiety, the type of all violence. Then, filled with disgust for everything, man will no longer feel either admiration or love for the world. He will turn away from this beautiful work, the most perfect alike in the present, the past, and the future. Nor will the languor and weariness of souls permit anything to remain save disdain of the whole universe, this immutable work of God, this glorious and perfect edifice, this manifold synthesis of forms and images, wherein the will of the Lord, lavish of marvels, has united all things in a harmonious and single whole, worthy for ever of veneration, of praise and love! Then darkness will be preferred to light, and death will be deemed better than life, nor will any man lift his eyes to heaven.

In those days the religious man will be thought mad; the impious man will be hailed as a sage; savage men will be deemed valiant; the evil-hearted will be applauded as the best of men. The Soul, and all that belongs thereto - whether born mortal or able to attain eternal life - all those things which I have herein expounded to thee, will be but matters for ridicule, and will be esteemed foolishness. There will even be peril of death, believe me, for those who remain faithful to religion and intelligence. New rights will be instituted, new laws, nor will there be left one holy word, one sacred belief, religious and worthy of heaven and of celestial things. O lamentable separation between the Gods and men! Then there will remain only evil demons who will mingle themselves with the miserable human race, their hand will be upon it impelling to all kinds of wicked enterprise; to war, to rapine, to falsehood, to everything contrary to the nature of the soul. The earth will no longer be in equilibrium, the sea will no longer be navigable, in the heavens the regular course of the stars will be troubled. Every holy voice will be condemned to silence; the fruits of the earth will become corrupt, and she will be no more fertile; the very air will sink into lugubrious torpor. Such will be the old age of the world; irreligion and disorder, lawlessness, and the confusion of good men.

When all these things shall be accomplished, O Asclepios, then the Lord and Father, the sovereign God who rules the wide world, beholding the evil ways and actions of men, will arrest these misfortunes by the exercise of His divine will and goodness. And, in order to put an end to error and to the general corruption, He will drown the world with a deluge or consume it by fire, or destroy it by wars and epidemics, and thereafter He will restore to it its primitive beauty; so that once more it shall appear worthy of admiration and worship, and again a chorus of praise and of blessing shall celebrate Him Who has created and redeemed so beautiful a work. This re-birth of the world, this restoration of all good things, this holy and sacred re-habilitation of Nature will take place when the time shall come which is appointed by the divine and ever-eternal will of God, without beginning and always the same.

Asclepios:

Indeed, Trismegistos, the nature of God is Will reflected; that is, absolute goodness and wisdom.

Hermes:

O Asclepios, Will is the result of reflection, and to will is itself an act of willing. For He Who is the fulness of all things and Who possesses all that He will, wills nothing by caprice. But everything He wills is good, and He has all that He wills; all that is good He thinks and wills. Such is God, and the World is the image of His righteousness.

Asclepios:

Is the world then good, O Trismegistos?

Hermes:

Yes, the world is good, Asclepios, as I will inform thee. Even as God accords to all beings and to all orders in the world benefits of divers kinds, such as thought, soul, and life, so likewise the world itself divides and distributes good things among mortals, changing seasons, the fruits of the earth, birth, increase, maturity, and other similar gifts. And thus God is above the summit of heaven, yet everywhere present and beholding all things. For beyond the heavens is a sphere without stars, transcending all corporeal things. Between heaven and earth he reigns who is the dispenser of life, and whom we call Zeus (Jupiter). Over the earth and the sea he reigns who nourishes all mortal creatures, the plants and fruit-bearing trees, and whose name is Zeus Sarapis (Jupiter Plutonius). And those to whom it shall be given to dominate the earth shall be sent forth and established at the extremity of Egypt, in a city built towards the west, whither, by sea and by land, shall flow all the race of mortals.

Asclepios:

But where are they now, Trismegistos?

Hermes:

They are established in a great city, upon the mountain of Lybia. Enough of this. [2]

Footnotes

1 Hermes speaks of the Stars, and of the Astral Powers, not of the Divine Intelligences. The whole of this discourse has a hidden and profound meaning, relating to the human organism, and to the elemental genii, which through man are individualised. A.K.

2 By "Egypt" is denoted not only the country of that name, but the physical system generally of the world, and especially - as in the Hebrew Scriptures - the human body.

PART X

Hermes:

Let us speak now of that which is immortal and of that which is mortal. The multitude, ignorant of the reason of things, is troubled by the approach and the fear of death. Death occurs by the dissolution of the body, wearied with its toil. When the number which maintains unity is complete –for the binding-power of the body is a number - the body dies. And this happens when it can no longer support the burdens of life. Such, then, is death; the dissolution of the body, and the end of corporeal sensations. It is superfluous to trouble oneself about such a matter. But there remains another necessary law which human ignorance and unbelief despise.

Asclepios:

What law is this which is thus ignored or unregarded?

Hermes:

Hearken, O Asclepios. When the soul is separated from the body, she passes under the supreme power of Deity, to be judged according to her merits. If found pious and just she is allowed to dwell in the divine abodes, but if she appears defiled with vice she is precipitated from height to depth, and delivered over to the tempests and adverse hurricanes of the air, the fire, and the water. Ceaselessly tossed about between heaven and earth by the billows of the universe, she is driven from side to side in eternal penance, her immortal nature gives endless duration to the judgment pronounced against her.[1] How greatly must we fear so dreadful a fate! They who now refuse to believe in such things will then be convinced against their will, not by words, but by beholding; not by menaces, but by the pains they will endure.

Asclepios:

The faults of men, O Trismegistos, are not then punished only by human laws?

Hermes:

O Asclepios, all that is terrestrial is mortal. Those who live according to the corporeal state, and who fall short during their life of the laws imposed on this condition, are subjected after death to chastisement so much the more severe as the faults committed by them have remained hidden; for the universal prescience of God will render the punishment proportional to the transgression.[2]

Asclepios:

Who are they who deserve the greatest penalties, O Trismegistos?

Hermes:

Those who, condemned by human laws, die a violent death, in such wise that they appear not to have paid the debt they owe to Nature, but to have received only the reward of their actions.³ The just man, on the contrary, finds in religion and in piety a great help, and God protects him against all evils. The Father and Lord of all things, Who alone is all, manifests Himself willingly to all; not that He shows any man His abode, nor His splendour, nor His greatness, but He enlightens man by intelligence alone, whereby the darkness of error is dissipated, and the glories of the truth revealed. By such means man is united to the Divine Intelligence; aspiring thither he is delivered from the mortal part of his nature, and conceives the hope of everlasting life. Herein is the difference between the good and the wicked. He who is illumined by piety, religion, wisdom, the service and veneration of God, sees, as with open eyes, the true reason of things; and, through the confidence of this faith, surpasses other men even as the sun the other fires of heaven. For if the sun enlightens the rest of the stars, it is not so much by his greatness and power as by his divinity and sanctity. Thou must see in him, O Asclepios, a secondary God, who rules the rest of the world, and illumines all its inhabitants, animate and inanimate.

If the world is an animated being which is, which has been, and which will be always living, nothing in it is mortal. Each of its parts is alive, for in a single creature always living there is no room for death. Thus is God the plenitude of life and of eternity, for He necessarily lives eternally; the sun is lasting as the universe, and governs perpetually all living creatures, being the fount and distributor of all vitality. God is, then, the ever-lasting Ruler of all things which receive life, and of all that give it, the eternal dispenser of the being of the universe. Now, He has once for all bestowed life on all living creatures by an immutable law which I will expound to thee. The movement of the universe is the life of eternity; the sphere of this motion is the eternity of life. The universe will never cease from movement, nor will it ever become corrupt; the permanence of eternal life surrounds it and protects it as a rampart. It dispenses life to all that is in its bosom; it is the bond of all things ordained under the sun. The effect of its motion is double; it is vivified by the eternity which encompasses it, and, in its turn, it vivifies all that it contains, diversifying everything according to certain fixed and determined numbers and seasons. All things are ordained in time by the action of the sun and the stars, according to a Divine law. Terrestrial periods are distinguished by the condition of the atmosphere, by the alternatives of heat and cold; celestial periods by the revolutions of the constellations, which return at fixed intervals of time to the same places in the heavens. The universe is the stage of time, the course and movement of which maintain Life. Order and time produce the renewal of all things in the world by recurring seasons.

Footnotes

1 This passage resembles a fragment of Empedocles, cited by Plutarch: - "The etherial force pursues them towards the sea, the sea vomits them forth upon its shores, the earth in turn flings them upward to the untiring sun, and the sun again drives them back into the whirl-wind of space. Thus all the elements toss them from one to another, and all hold them in horror." [It is needless to add that the whole of this passage is allegorical, and that the penance referred to is that of Purgatory, or Kama Loka - the intermediate state of purification.]

2 This passage qualifies the previous statement in Sect. IX., concerning the duration of the purgatorial state, and shows that it is not to be regarded as eternal, but as proportional to the faults committed. Moreover, it supplies a reason for the Catholic custom of shriving the dying, seeing that unconfessed sin entails heavier penalty than sin confessed, and therefore no longer "hidden."

3 An obscure passage. Probably its meaning is that great sinners, cut off by violent means in the midst of their iniquity, have no time to work out their penance in life, and, being thus deprived of the opportunity of restitution and amendment, suffer the more acutely in purgatory. For since they cannot discharge their debt on earth, they are delivered to torment after death until the "uttermost farthing" is paid.

A.K.

[The opinions expressed in the above, or other scholarly annotations herein, must be disclaimed being in any way necessarily accepted as expressive of, or identical with my own.

Robt. H. Fryar, Bath.]

PART XI

Since such is the state of the universe, there is nothing immutable, nothing stable, nothing unchanging in nature, either in the heavens or on the earth. God alone, and rightly alone, is wholly full and perfect in Himself, of Himself, and around Himself. He is His own firm stability, nor can He be moved by any impulsion, since all things are in Him, and He alone is all. Unless, indeed, we should dare to say, that His movement is in eternity, but this eternity itself is motionless, since all the motion of time revolves in eternity and takes its form therein. God, then, has ever been and is for ever immutable; with Him likewise is the immutable eternity, bearing within it, as the image of

God, the uncreated universe not yet manifest. Hence, the created universe constitutes the imitation of this eternal universe. Time, despite its perpetual movement, possesses, by means of its necessary revolutions on itself, the force and nature of stability. Thus, although eternity is fixed and immutable, nevertheless, since the motion of time unfolds itself in eternity, and this mobility is the very condition of time, it appears that eternity, immutable in itself, yet revolves by means of the time which is within it, and which contains all motion. Thence it results that the stability of eternity appears mobile, and the mobility of time, stable, by the fixed law of their course. And thus it might seem even that God moves in His own immutability. For there is in the immensity of the equilibrium an unchangeable movement; the law of His immensity is unchangeable.

That, therefore, which is not subject to sense - the Infinite, the Incomprehensible, the Immeasureable - can not be sustained, nor carried, nor sought out; neither can we know whence it comes, whither it goes, where it is, how it is, nor what it is. It is contained in its own supreme stability, and its stability in it; whether God be in eternity, or eternity in God, or both one and the other in the two. Eternity is undefinable by time; and time, which may be defined by number, by alternative, or by periodical revolutions, is eternal. Thus both appear equally infinite and eternal. Stability being the fixed point which serves as the basis of Movement, must, because of this stability, hold the principal place. God and Eternity are, therefore, the principle of all things; but the world, which is mutable, cannot be considered the principle. The mutability of the world takes precedence of its stability, by means of the law of eternal movement in equilibrium. The whole consciousness of Divinity is then immutable, and moves only in equilibrium; it is holy, incorruptible, eternal; or to define it better, it is eternity, consisting in the very truth of the Supreme God, the plenitude of all feeling and knowledge, or indeed, so to speak, in God Himself. The consciousness of the natural universe includes all sensible things and species; the consciousness of humanity involves memory, by which man remembers his acts performed.

Now, the consciousness of Divinity descends even to the human creature. God has not seen fit to extend to all beings this supreme and divine consciousness, lest, were it common to all animals, the glory of it should be diminished. The intelligence of the human mind, - whatever may be its quality and quantity, - lies wholly in the memory, and it is by means of this tenacity of memory that man has become the lord of the earth. The intelligence of nature, the quality and consciousness of the universe, may be understood by means of the sensible things it contains. Eternity, in the next place, is understood as to its consciousness and its quality, according to the sensible world.

But the intelligence of the Divine Being, the consciousness of the Supreme God, is the only truth, and this truth cannot be discovered, - no, nor so much as its shadow, - in this world full of illusion, of changeful appearances, and of error, where things are known only in the dimension of time.

Thou seest, O Asclepios, what lofty matters we dare to treat! I thank Thee, O most high God, Who hast illumined me with the light of Thy Grace! As for you, O Tat, Asclepios, and Ammon, keep these Divine mysteries in the secret place of your hearts, and conceal them in silence. Intellect differs from perception in this - that intellect, by means of study, is competent to understand and to know the nature of the universe.

The intellect of the universe penetrates to the consciousness of eternity, and of the super-mundane Gods. And as for us who are men, we perceive heavenly things as it were darkly through a mist, for thus only does the condition of our human sense

permit us to behold them. Feeble, indeed, is our strength to penetrate things so Divine; but, when at last we attain to them, we are indeed blessed by the joy of our inward consciousness.

PART XII

Concerning the Void, to which so much importance is attached, my judgment is that it does not exist, that it never has existed, and that it never will exist. For all the various parts of the universe are filled, as the earth also is complete and full of bodies, differing in quality and in form, having their species and their magnitude, one larger, one smaller, one solid, one tenuous. The larger and more solid are easily perceived; the smaller and more tenuous are difficult to apprehend, or altogether invisible. We know only of their existence by the sensation of feeling, wherefore many persons deny such entities to be bodies, and regard them as simply spaces, but it is impossible there should be such spaces. For if indeed there should be anything outside the universe, which I do not believe, then it would be a space occupied by intelligible beings analogous to its Divinity, in such wise that the world, which we call the sensible world, would be filled with bodies and creatures appropriate to its nature and quality. We do not behold all the aspects of the world; some of these indeed are very vast, others very small, or else they appear small to us by reason of their remoteness, or the imperfection of our sight; their extreme tenuity may even cause us to be wholly ignorant of their existence. I speak of the genii, for I hold they dwell with us, and of the heroes who dwell above us, between the earth and the higher airs; wherein are neither clouds nor any tempest.

For in truth, O Asclepios, it cannot be said that there is anywhere a void, unless care be taken to define what is signified by void; as, for instance, void of fire, or water, or of some other such thing. And even if this or that space, small or great, be empty of these elements, nothing can be empty of the spirit and aerial fluid. The same thing may be said of place; this word alone cannot be understood, unless it is applied to something. By omitting the chief term, the sense intended is lost; thus, it is correct to say, "the place of water," "the place of fire," or of any other similar thing. For as it is impossible that there should be space void of everything, so also it is impossible there should be place by itself. If a place is supposed without its contents, then it is an empty place, and, in my judgment, such a place does not exist in the universe. But if nothing be void, then there can be no such thing as place in itself, unless it be qualified by length, breadth, and depth, even as human bodies have distinguishing signs.

If, then, these things be so, O Asclepios and you who are also present, know that the Intelligible World, that is to say, God, Who is perceived only by the eye of intelligence, is incorporeal, and that nothing corporeal can be mingled with His nature, nor anything that can be defined by quality, quantity, or numeration, for there is nothing of such a kind in Him. This world, which is called the sensible world, is the receptacle of all sensible appearances, qualities, and bodies, nor can this universe exist without God. For God is all, and all come forth from Him, and depend on His Will; He contains everything that is good, orderly, wise, perfect, perceptible for Him alone, and intelligible for Him alone. Apart from Him nothing has been, nothing is, nothing will be; for all proceed from Him, are in Him, and by Him; whether manifold qualities, vast quantities, magnitudes exceeding measurement, species of all forms. If thou understandest these things, Asclepios, render thanks to God; and, observing the universe, comprehend clearly that this sensible world, and all that it contains, is enfolded, as in a garment, by the supernal world. O Asclepios, beings of every kind, whether mortals, immortals, reasonable, animate, inanimate, to whatever class they may belong, bear the impress of that class, and although each of them has the general appearance of its kind, there are yet among them special differences. Even so, the human kind is uniform, and man may be defined by his type; nevertheless, under this general likeness, men present many dissimilarities. For the character which proceeds from God is incorporeal, as is all that is comprehended in intelligence. Since the two principles which determine form are corporeal and incorporeal, it is impossible that they should generate a form wholly resembling something else, at whatever distance of time or of place. Forms, nevertheless, are as changeful as the moments in an hour's space, in the moveable circle wherein is that omniform God of whom we have spoken. Therefore the type persists, producing as many images of itself as the revolution of the world has instants of time. The world has changes in its revolution, but species (individuality) has neither period nor change. Thus the forms of every species are permanent, and yet various in the same species.

Asclepios:

And does the world also vary in its species, Trismegistos?

Hermes:

Why then, Asclepios, hast thou been asleep all the while we have been discoursing? What is the world, or of what is it composed, if not of all that is generated in it? Or dost thou speak of heaven, of the earth, and of the elements, for other beings continually change in appearance? But even so the heaven, now rainy, now dry, now hot, now cold, now clear, now covered with clouds, has many successive changes of aspect beneath its apparent uniformity. So also the earth constantly changes its aspect, for now it brings forth its fruits, now it hides them in its bosom, bearing products of diverse quality and quantity; here is repose, there is movement, and every variety of trees, flowers, seeds, properties, odours, savours, forms. Fire, likewise, has its manifold and divine transformations, for the sun and the moon have all manner of aspects comparable to the multitude of images beheld in mirrors. And now we have discoursed enough of these things.

PART XIII

Let us return to man, and enquire concerning the divine gift of reason which entitles him to be called a reasonable creature. Among all the wonders we have noted in man, that which above all commands admiration is this: - that man has discovered the divinity of nature, and has made it efficient to his designs. [1]

Our ancestors, wandering astray in matters of faith concerning the Gods, and unable to lift their minds to the Divine knowledge and religion, discovered the art of making Gods; and, having discovered it, they invested their products with appropriate virtues drawn from the nature of the world. And, as they could not make souls, they evoked the spirits of genii and angels, and endowed with them the holy images and sacraments, thus enabling their idols to exercise powers for good or ill. In such wise thine ancestor, O Asclepios, the inventor of medicine, has a temple on the Lybian mountain by the shores of the crocodile-frequented river, where also lies enshrined all of him which belonged to the earth - that is, his body. For the rest of him - his better part, or rather, indeed, himself - because the principle of consciousness and of life is the whole man - is restored to heaven. And now, by his divinity, he lends help to men in their sicknesses, who once instructed them in the art of healing. So also, Hermes, my own ancestor, whose name I bear, now enshrined in the country which is called after him, hears the prayers of those who come thither from all parts of the land to obtain of him assistance and health. Behold, again, what blessings Isis, the spouse of Osiris, confers upon men when she is favourable to them, and what ills she inflicts when she is angered! For these mundane and earthly Gods are accessible to wrath, being formed and composed by men out of Nature. Of, such sort in Egypt is the adoration paid to animals; and thus also do cities honour the souls of those men who, in their lifetime, gave them laws and whose names they preserve. And for this reason, O Asclepios, those deities which are adored in some places, receive in others no worship; whence arise many wars between the cities of Egypt.

Asclepios:

And of what kind, O Trismegistos, is the divinity of these Gods who inhabit the earth?

Hermes:

It consists in the divine virtue, which naturally subsists in herbs, rocks, and aromatic principles, wherefore these deities love frequent sacrifices, hymns, and praises, and sweet music resembling the celestial harmony, which heaven-like rite, attractive to their sacred nature, draws them and retains them in their shrines, so that they patiently endure their long sojourn among men. It is thus that men make Gods. Neither must thou suppose, O Asclepios, that the acts of these terrestrial deities are controlled by hazard. For while the supernal Gods abide in the heights of heaven, keeping each the order which belongs to him, these Gods of ours have also their special functions. Some predict by means of lots and divination the events of the future; others preside, in various ways, over things depending on their care, or come to our assistance as allies, as kinsmen, or as friends.

Footnotes

1 This section continues and elucidates the argument of section IX. An acquaintance with occult doctrine regarding the Nature-spirits, or mundane Gods, will, I think, enable the reader to follow intelligently the observations of Hermes in regard to the sacred images. Precisely the same virtues as those attributed by the ancients to the idols of their various deities, are in our day attributed by Catholics to the idols of their saints. We hear of the "Virgin" of

this or that town being propitious to a petition which the "Virgin" of some other place has refused to grant. Sacred images still heal the sick, avert pestilences, discover hidden springs, and confer blessings upon devotees. Hermes points out that the powers by which these things are accomplished belong to the divinity of Nature, individualised and differentiated by human intervention; and that mankind necessarily passes through the stage of nature-worship before becoming competent to realise the celestial order and the being of the heavenly Gods. For before the empyrean can be reached by the human intelligence, it must traverse the spheres intermediate between earth and heaven. Thus the images of the Gods are worshipped before the Gods themselves are known; nor are these images necessarily of wood or stone. All personalities are eidola (idols) reflecting the true essentials, and having, as it were, a portion of Divinity attached to them and resident in their forms, but none the less are they images, and however powerful and adorable they may appear to the multitude who know not divine religion, they are to the Hermetist but types and persona of essentials which are eternally independent of manifestation and unaffected by it. The signs of the truly Divine are three: transcendency of form, transcendency of time, transcendency of personality. Instead of form is Essence; instead of time, Eternity; instead of persons, Principles. Events become Processes, and phenomena, Noumena. So long as the conception of any divine idea remains associated with, or dependent on, any physical or historical circumstance, so long it is certain that the heavenly plane has not been reached. Symbols, when they are recognised as symbols, are no longer either deceptive or dangerous; they are merely veils of light rendering visible the "Divine Dark," towards which the true Hermetist aspires. Even the most refined, the subtlest and most metaphysical expression of the supreme Truth is still symbol and metaphor, for the Truth itself is unutterable, save by God to God. It is Essence, Silence, Darkness.

A.K.

PART XIV

Asclepios:
O Trismegistos, what is the part taken in the order of things by Destiny or Fate? If the heavenly Gods rule the universe, and the mundane deities control special events, where is the part of Destiny?

Hermes:
O Asclepios, Destiny is the necessity which compels all things that happen, the chain which binds together all events. It is thus the cause of

things, the supreme deity, or rather the second God created by God, that is the law of all things in heaven and earth established upon divine ordinances. Destiny and Necessity are bound together indissolubly: Destiny produces the beginning of all things, Necessity enforces the effect which ensues from these beginnings. And hence arises Order - that is, the sequence and disposition of things accomplished in Time; for nothing is performed without Order. And thus the world is perfected; for the world is founded on Order, and in Order the universe consists. Therefore these three, Destiny (which is Fate), Necessity, and Order, depend absolutely on the will of God Who governs the world by His divine law and reason. These three principles have no will in themselves; inflexible and inaccessible to favour as to anger, they are but the instruments of the eternal Reason, which is immutable, invariable, unalterable, indissoluble. First comes Destiny, containing, like newly-sown soil, the germs of future events. Necessity follows, urging them to their consummation. Lastly, Order maintains the fabric of things established by Destiny and Necessity. For all this is an ever-lasting sequence without beginning or end, sustained by its immutable law in the continuity of eternity. It rises and falls alternately, and as time rolls onward, that which had disappeared, again rises uppermost. For such is the condition of the circular movement; all things are interchained in such wise that neither beginning nor end can be distinguished, and they appear to precede and follow each other unceasingly. But as for accident and chance, they pervade all mundane affairs.

PART XV

And now, inasmuch as it is given to man, and inasmuch as God has permitted, we have spoken concerning everything; it re-mains only, therefore, that we should bless and pray to God and return to our mortal cares, having satisfied our minds by treating of sacred things which are the food of the mind.

Therewith, coming forth from the Sanctuary, they addressed to God their oraisons, turning themselves to the south, because when the sun begins to decline, he who would praise the God should direct his gaze thither, as in like manner, at sunrise, he should look towards the orient. And even while they pronounced their invocations, Asclepios, in a low voice, spoke thus:

O Tatius, let us ask our father that our prayers may be accompanied with odours of incense and perfumes.

Trismegistos heard, and was moved.

May the omen be favourable, O Asclepios, he said. It is almost a sacrilege to burn incense or any other perfume during prayer; He Who is all and Who contains all, desires nothing. Let us give Him praise and adoration only; the divinest odours are acts of grace which mortals render to God.

We give Thee thanks, O Lord Most High, for by Thy grace we have received the light of Thy knowledge; may Thy Name be adored and venerated, only Name by which Deity is praised according to the religion of our fathers! For Thou dost vouchsafe to accord to all of us the ancestral faith, piety, love, and the most worthy and gracious gifts, in that Thou bestowest upon us consciousness, reason, and intelligence. By consciousness we discern Thee, by reason we seek Thee, and intelligence endows us with the joy of understanding Thee. Saved by Thy divine power, let us be glad in beholding the manifestation of Thyself; let us be glad that, from the hour of our sojourn in the body, Thou dost deign to consecrate us to eternity. The only joy of Man is the knowledge of Thy majesty. We have known Thee, O magnificent Light, who art apprehended by Intelligence alone! We have known Thee, O true Way of Life, inexhaustible Source of all births! We have known Thee, O generative Plenitude of all Nature, Eternal Permanence! And in this our oraison, adoring the sanctity of Thy holiness, we ask of Thee only to grant that we may persevere in the love of Thy knowledge, in such wise that we may never separate ourselves from this manner of life. With which hope being filled, we go forth to take a pure repast without animal flesh. [1]

Footnotes

1 The words with which this Discourse on Initiation ends are full of significance. The key to the Hermetic Secret is found when the aspirant adopts the Edenic Life: the life of purity and charity which all mystics - Hebrew, Egyptian, Buddhist, Greek, Latin, Vedic, with one consent, ascribe to man in the golden age of his primeval perfection. The first outcome of the Fall, or Degeneracy, is the shedding of blood and eating of flesh. The license to kill is the sign-manual of "Paradise Lost." And the first step towards "Paradise Regained" is taken when man voluntarily returns to the manner of life indicated by his organism as that alone befitting him, and thus reunites himself to the harmony of Nature and the Will of God. No man who follows this path and faithfully keeps to it will fail to find at length the Gate of Paradise. Not necessarily in a single life-time, for the process of purification is a long one, and the past experiences of some men may be such as to shut them out for many lives from the attainment of the promised land. But, nevertheless, every step faithfully and firmly trodden, brings them nearer to the goal, every year of pure life increasingly strengthens the spirit, purges the mind, liberates the will, and augments their human royalty. On the

other hand, it is idle to seek union with God in the Spirit, while the physical and magnetic organism remains insurgent against Nature. Harmony must be established between man and Nature before union can be accomplished between man and God. For Nature is the manifest God; and if man be not in perfect charity with that which is visible, how shall he love that which is invisible? Hermetic doctrine teaches the kinship and solidarity of all beings, redeemed and glorified in man. For man does not stand aloof and apart from other creatures, as though he were a fallen angel dropped from some supernal world upon the earth, but he is the child of earth, the product of evolution, the elder brother of all conscient things; their lord and king, but not their tyrant. It is his part to be to all creatures a Good Destiny; he is the keeper, the redeemer, the regenerator of the earth. If need be, he may call on his subjects to serve him as their king, but he may never, without forfeiting his kingship, maltreat and afflict them. All the children of God, in every land and age, have abstained from blood, in obedience to an occult law which asserts itself in the breast of all regenerate men. The mundane Gods are not averse to blood, for by means of it they are invigorated and enabled to manifest. For the mundane Gods are the forces of the astral element in man, which element dominates in the unregenerate. Therefore, the unregenerate are under the power of the stars, and subject to illusion. Inasmuch as a man is clean from the defilement of blood, insomuch he is less liable to be beguiled by the deceptions of the astral serpent. Therefore, let all who seek the Hermetic secret, do their utmost to attain to the Hermetic life. If entire abstinence from all forms of animal food be impossible, let a lower degree be adopted, admitting the use of the least bloody meats only - milk, fish, eggs, and the flesh of birds. But in such a case, let the intention of the aspirant be continually united with that of Nature, willing with firm desire to lead, whenever possible, a yet more perfect life; so that in a future birth he may be enabled to attain to it.

A.K.

END OF THE TREATISE ON INITIATIONS

BOOK III
THE DEFINITIONS
OF ASCLEPIOS

PART I

Asclepios to the King Ammon.

I address to thee, O King, a comprehensive discourse,[1] which is, as it were, the sum and epitome of all others. Far from being in accordance with the opinion of the vulgar, it is wholly adverse thereto. Even to thee, it may seem inconsistent with certain of my discourses. My master, Hermes, who frequently conversed with me, either alone, or in the presence of Tatios, was wont to say that those who should read my writings would affirm their doctrine to be quite simple and clear, while indeed, on the contrary, it is truly occult and contains a hidden sense. And it has become yet more obscure since the Greeks undertook to translate it from our language into theirs. This has been a source of difficulty and perversion of sense. The character of the Egyptian language, and the energy of the words it uses, enforce the meaning on the mind. As much then as thou canst, O King, and indeed thou art all-powerful, prevent this discourse from being translated, lest these mysteries should reach the Greeks, and their manner of speech, adorned and elegant in expression, should, perchance, weaken the vigour and diminish the solemn gravity and force of these words. The Greeks, O King, have new forms of language for producing argument, and their philosophy is prodigal of speech. We, on the other hand, employ not words so much as the great language of facts.

I will begin this discourse by invoking God, the Master of the Universe, the Creator and the Father, Who contains all, Who is All in One, and One in All. For the plenitude of all things is Unity, and in Unity; nor is the one term inferior to the other, since the two are one. Bear in mind this thought, O King, during the whole of my exposition. Vain is it to seek to distinguish the All and the One by designating the multitude of things the All, and not their Plenitude. Such a distinction is impossible, for the All exists no longer if separated from Unity; and if Unity exists, it is in the Totality; now it indeed exists and never ceases to be One, otherwise the Plenitude would be dissolved.

In the bosom of the earth there are impetuous springs of water and of fire; such are the three natures of fire, water, and earth, proceeding from a common origin. Whereby it may be thought that there is one general fountain of matter, bringing forth all abundantly and receiving existence from on high. It is thus that heaven and earth are governed by their creator, that is, by the sun, who causes essence to stream downwards, and matter to rise upwards, and who draws to himself the universe, giving all to everything, lavish of the benefits of his radiance. It is he who distributes beneficent energies not only in heaven and throughout the air, but upon earth also, and even in the depths of the abyss. If there be an intelligible substance, it must be the very substance of the sun, whose light is the vehicle thereof. But what may be its constitution and primal fount, he only knows. That by induction we may understand that which is hidden from our sight, it would be necessary to be near him and analogous to his nature. But that which he permits us to behold is no conjecture; it is the splendid vision which illuminates the universal and supernal world.

In the midst of the universe is the sun established, like the bearer of the crowns; and even as a skilful driver, he directs and maintains the chariot of the world, holding it to its course. He keeps fast the reins of it, even life, soul, spirit, immortality, and birth. He drives it before him, or, rather, with him. And after this manner he forms all things, dispensing to immortals eternal permanence. The light, which from his outer part streams towards heaven, nourishes the immortal spaces of the universe. The rest, encircling and illuminating the entirety of the waters, the earth, and the air, becomes the matrix wherein life germinates, wherein are initiated all births and metamorphoses, transforming creatures, as by a spiral motion, and causing them to pass from one portion of the world to another, from one species to another, and from one appearance to another; maintaining the equilibrium of their mutual metamorphoses, as in the creation of greater entities. For the permanence of bodies consists in transmutation. But immortal forms are indissoluble, and mortal bodies decompose; such is the difference between the immortal and the mortal.

This creation of life by the sun is as continuous as his light; nothing arrests or limits it. Around him, like an army of satellites, are innumerable choirs of Genii. These dwell in the neighbourhood of the Immortals, and thence watch over human things. They fulfil the will of the Gods by means of storms, tempests, transitions of fire, and earthquakes; likewise by famines and wars, for the punishment of impiety. For the greatest crime of men is impiety towards the Gods. The nature of the Gods is to do good, the duty of men is to be pious, the function of the Genii is to chastise. The Gods do not hold men responsible for faults committed through mistake or boldness, by that necessity which belongs to fate, or by ignorance; only iniquity falls under the weight of their justice.

It is the sun who preserves and nourishes all creatures; and even as the Ideal World which environs the sensible world fills this last with the plenitude and universal variety of forms, so also the sun enfolding all in his light accomplishes everywhere the birth and development of creatures, and when they fall wearied in the race, gathers them again to his bosom. Under his orders is the choir of the Genii, or rather the choirs, for there are many and diverse, and their number corresponds to that of the stars. Every star has its genii, good and evil by nature, or rather by their operation, for operation is

the essence of the genii. I n some there is both good and evil operation. All
. these Genii preside over mundane affairs, they shake and overthrow the constitution of States and of individuals; they imprint their likeness on our souls, they are present in our nerves, our marrow, our veins, our arteries, and our very brain-substance, and in the recesses of our viscera. At the moment when each of us receives life and being, he is taken in charge by the genii who preside over births, and who are classed beneath the astral powers. Perpetually they change, not always identical, but revolving in circles. They permeate by the body two parts of the soul, that it may receive from each the impress of his own energy. But the reasonable part of the soul is not subject to the genii; it is designed for the reception of God, who enlightens it with a sunny ray. Those who are thus illumined are few in number, and from them the genii abstain; for neither genii nor gods have any power in the presence of a single ray of God. But all other men, both soul and body, are directed by genii, to whom they cleave, and whose operations they affect. But reason is not like desire, which deceives and misleads. The genii, then, have the control of mundane things, and our bodies serve them as instruments. Now, it is this control which Hermes calls Destiny. [2]

The Intelligible World is attached to God, the Sensible World to the Intelligible World, and through these two worlds, the sun conducts the effluence of God, that is, the creative energy. Around him are the eight spheres which are bound to him - the sphere of the fixed stars, the six spheres of the planets, and that which surrounds the earth. To these spheres the genii are bound, and to the genii, men; and thus are all beings bound to God, who is the universal Father. The sun is the creator; the world is the crucible of creation. The Intelligible Essence rules heaven, heaven directs the gods, under these are classed the genii, who guide mankind. Such is the divine hierarchy, and such is the operation which God accomplishes by gods and genii for Himself. Everything is a part of God, thus God is all. In creating all, He perpetuates Himself without any intermission, for the energy of God has no past, and since God is without limits, His creation is without beginning or end. [3]

Footnotes

1 This discourse, which usually concludes, not precedes, the "Fragments," is sometimes but erroneously attributed to Apuleius; see Hargrave Jennings' scholarly and exhaustive "Introductory Essay" to my Annotated Edition of "The Divine Pymander."
Robt. H. Fryar, Bath.

2 Asclepios, throughout this discourse, preaches pure Hermetic doctrine, which discourages all traffic with elementals, astrals, and other dæmonic

influences, whether beneficent or the reverse, and instructs man rather to seek the grace of the Holy Spirit, by aspiring evermore inwards and upwards, and abiding in the reasonable and divine part of his nature.

3 Compare with this declaration the opening passage of Section III. in the Book of Hermes to Tatios, and my note thereon. The Divine Olympos, or Mount of Energies, emits a continuous river of Generation, or "Becoming." And the equilibrium of Nature is continually maintained by a corresponding process of perpetual return from Matter to Essence; from Existence to Being. With the right hand ADONAI projects; with the left He indraws.

The leading idea in the above fragment is the parallelism between Man and the Universe. The whole Solar System of the Macrocosm, with its hierarchy of gods and elemental powers, is resumed in the human system of the Microcosm.

A.K.

PART II

If thou reflectest, O King, thou wilt perceive that there are incorporeal corporealites. Which are they? says the King. Corporealites which appear in mirrors; are they not incorporeal?

It is true, Tat, says the King; thou hast a marvellous fancy!

There are yet other incorporealities; for instance, abstract forms, what say you to them? Are they not in themselves incorporeal? yet they are manifest in animated and inanimated corporealities.

True again, Tat.

So then there is a reflexion of incorporealities upon corporealities, and of corporealities on incorporealities. In other words, the Sensible World and the Ideal World reflect each other. Adore, then, the sacred images, O King, for they also are reflective forms of the Sensible World.

Then the King rose and said, Methinks, prophet, it is time to look after our guests; to-morrow, we can continue this theological controversy. [1]

Footnotes

1 As I read the above fragment, it is written in a spirit of mirth. Tat is quibbling with the King, as the manner of their talk plainly shows. Nevertheless, an undercurrent of occult meaning runs through the speech of the son of Trismegistos. When he names the sacred images, the allusion intended is to the cultus of the Mysteries. - A.K.

PART III

When a musician, desiring to conduct a melody, is hindered in his design by the want of accord in the instruments employed, his efforts end in ridicule, and provoke the laughter of the auditors. In vain he expends the resources of his art, or accuses of falseness the instrument which reduces him to impotence.

The great musician of Nature, the God who presides over the harmony of song, and who controls the resonance of the instruments according to the rhythm of the melody, is unwearying, for weariness reaches not the gods. And if an artist conducts a concert of music, and the trumpeters blow according to their ability, the flute-players express the delicate modulations of the melody, and the lyre and violin accompany the song, who would think of accusing the inspiration of the composer, or withhold from him the esteem his work deserves, if some instrument should trouble the melody with discord and hinder the auditors from seizing its purity? Even so, not without impiety can we impeach Humanity, on account of the impotence of our own body. For know that God is an Artist of untiring Spirit, always Master of His science, always successful in His operations, and everywhere bestowing equal benefits. If Phidias, the creative artisan, should find the material on which it is necessary for him to work, refractory to his skill, let us not blame him who has laboured to the utmost of his power; neither let us accuse the musician of the faults of the instrument, but rather complain of the defective chord, which, by lowering or raising a note, has destroyed the concord; and the worse this is, the more does he merit praise who succeeds in drawing from such a chord an accurate tone. Far from reproaching him, the auditors will be all the better pleased with him. It is thus, O most illustrious hearers, that our inward lyre must be attuned to the intention of the musician.

I can even imagine that a musician, deprived of the aid of his lyre, and being called upon to produce some great musical effect, might, by untried means, supply the place of the accustomed instrument, and arouse thereby the enthusiasm of his auditors. It is related of a cithara player, to whom Apollo was favourable, that, being once suddenly checked in his performance of a melody by the snapping of a string, the kindness of the God supplied the want and magnified the talent of the artist; for by providential help, a cicada interposed his song and executed the missing notes which the broken cord should have sounded. The musician, reassured, and no more troubled by the accident, obtained a triumph. I feel in myself, O most noble hearers, something similar; for, but now, being convinced of my incapacity and weakness, the power of the Supreme Being has supplied in my stead the melody wherewith to praise the king. For the design of this discourse is to declare the glory of royalties and their achievements. Forward, then! the musician wills it, and for this the lyre is tuned! May the grandeur and sweetness of the melody respond to the purpose of our song!

And since we have tuned our lyre to hymn the praise of kings, and to celebrate their renown, let us first praise the good God, the supreme King of the universe. After Him we will glorify those who reflect His image, and hold the sceptre of royalty. Kings themselves are glad that the song should descend from above, degree after degree, that aspiration should draw nigh to Heaven whence victory comes to them. Let, then, the singer praise the mighty God of the universe, ever immortal, whose power is eternal as Himself, the first of Victors, from Whom all triumphs come, succeeding one another. Let us hasten to close our discourse, that we may offer praise to kings, even to those who are the guardians of peace and of general security; who hold from the Lord supreme their ancient power, and receive victory from His hand; those whose sceptres shine resplendent to herald the hardships of war, whose triumphs anticipate the conflict; and to whom it is given not only to reign, but to overcome; whose very advance to battle strikes the barbarian enemy with fear.

PART IV

This discourse ends where it began, with the praise of the Supreme Being, and afterwards of the most holy kings by whom we obtain peace. So that having commenced by celebrating the Almighty greatness, it is to this greatness that we return in terminating our speech. Even as the sun nourishes all germs, and receives the promise of the fruits which his rays, like divine hands, gather for the God; even as these shining hands collect likewise the sweet odours of plants, so also we, after having begun by the adoration of the Most High and the effluence of His Wisdom, after having gathered into our souls the fragrance of these heavenly flowers, must now collect the sweetness of this sacred harvest which He, with fruitful rains, will bless. But even if we had ten thousand mouths and ten thousand voices wherewith to glorify the God of all purity, the Father of Souls, we should yet be powerless to celebrate Him worthily; for new-born babes cannot, indeed, rightly extol their father, yet since they do their utmost, they obtain indulgence. Or rather, the glory of God is seen in this, that He is superior to all creatures; He is the Beginning, He is the End, the Midst, and the Continuance of their Praise; in Him they acknowledge their Parent, all-powerful and infinite.

It is the same also with our king. We, who are his children, love to extol him; and we ask indulgence of our father, even when, before we asked, it was granted to us. A father, far from turning away from his little ones, and from his new-born infants, because of their feebleness, rejoices to see himself recognised by them. The universal gnosis which communicates life to all, and enables us to bless God, is itself a gift of God. For God, being good, has in Himself the fulness of all perfection; being immortal, He contains in Himself immortal tranquillity, and His eternal power sends forth into this world a salutary benediction. In the hierarchy which He contains there are no differences nor variations; all the beings in Him are wise, the same providence is in all, the same intelligence governs them, the same sentiment impels them to mutual goodness, and the same love produces among them universal harmony.

Therefore, let us bless God and after Him the kings who from Him receive the sceptre. And having inaugurated the praises of the kings, let us also glorify piety towards the Supreme. May He instruct us how to bless Him, and may His aid assist us in this study. May our first and chief endeavour be to celebrate the fear of God and the praise of the Kings. For to them is due our gratitude for the fruitful peace which by their means we enjoy. It is the virtue of the King, and his name only which obtains peace; he is called King because he advances chief in royalty and power, and because he reigns by reason and peace. He is above all barbarian royalties, his very name is a symbol of peace. The name alone of the King suffices often to repel the foe. His images are as beacons of safety in the tempest. For the very image of our King procures victory, confers security, and renders us invulnerable.

[Patrizzi hesitates to ascribe the fragment entitled "Asclepios to King Ammon" to the disciple of Hermes, thinking it unworthy of one who had enjoyed the instructions of so great a man. Dr. Menard points out that despite the tirade against the Greeks and the Greek tongue in the first section of this fragment, it was undoubtedly originally written in that very language, as is proved by the reference made in the third section, to the Greek word for 'the king', and the etymological derivation of the word (to advance), and also by the allusions to Phidias, and to Eunomios, a musician of Locris, in the second section. The description of the sun as a charioteer, and the passing reference to "him who bears the crowns," are also both suggested by Greek usages. In Egypt the sun was always represented as carried on a barge or floating raft along the waters of the Nile. Dr. Menard inclines, therefore, to

believe that the depreciatory remarks concerning the Greeks must have been introduced by a fraudulent hand, in order to mislead the reader in regard to the true origin of the fragment. Dr. Menard is, moreover, of opinion that the king, or kings spoken of in the fragment, are the imperial brothers Valens and Valentinian. I venture to differ from this view, and believe, rather, that the writer, whether indeed the true Asclepios or not, certainly uses the words "king," "kings," and "royalties" in an occult sense. For if he intended, as Dr. Menard supposes, a mere commonplace eulogium on a reigning monarch or monarchs - whether Ammon, or Valens and his brother - to what purpose should he set out by declaring his writings to be "truly occult and containing a hidden sense"? All that is said in the fragment concerning kingship is perfectly applicable to the mystic Osiris, the nature of whose royalty has been elsewhere explained. Osiris is the reflection and counterpart in Man, of the supreme Lord of the Universe, the ideal type of humanity; hence the soul, or essential ego, presenting itself for judgment in the spiritual world, is in the Egyptian Ritual of the Dead, described as "an Osiris." It is to this Osiris, or king within us, our higher Reason, the true Word of God, that we owe perpetual reverence, service, and faithful allegiance.]

A.K.

END OF THE DEFINITIONS

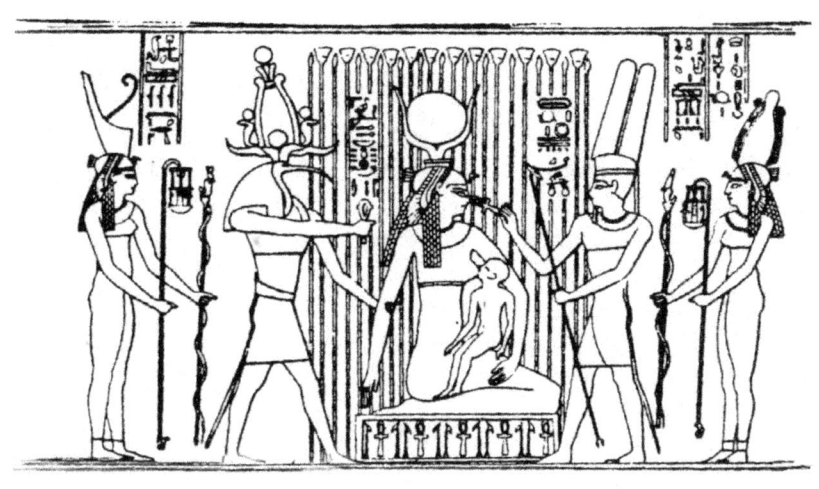

BOOK IV
FRAGMENTS

FRAGMENTS OF THE BOOK OF HERMES TO HIS SON TATIOS

PART I

Trismegistos.

It is for the love of men and for the veneration of God, O my son, that I begin to write this. For there is no other true religion than to meditate on the universe and give thanks to the Creator; and these things I shall not cease to do.

Tatios.

O father, if nothing here below be real, how can one wisely employ one's life?

Trismegistos.

Be religious, my son; religion is lofty philosophy; without philosophy there is no lofty religion. He who instructs himself concerning the universe, its law, its principle, and its end, gives thanks for all things to the Creator as to a gracious father, a good protector, a faithful teacher. This is religion, and by means of it we know where truth is and what it is. Knowledge increases religion. For when once the soul, imprisoned within the body, has lifted herself to the perception of the real Good and of Truth, she cannot again fall back. The might of Love, and the oblivion of all evil things, forbid the soul who knows her Maker to separate herself from the Good. Herein, my son, is the aim of religion; if thou canst attain thereunto, thy life will be pure, thy death happy; thy soul will know whither she ought to direct her flight. Herein is the only way which leads to Truth, which, indeed, our ancestors trod, and by which they arrived at the attainment of the Good. This way is beautiful and even; nevertheless, it is difficult for the soul to walk therein so long as she is immured within the prison of the body. For, first, she must contend against herself, and having accomplished a division of herself, she must submit to that part of herself which is first in dignity. For the one struggles against the two, that would fain rise, but these would drag it downwards.[1] Nor is victory the same to both sides; for the one tends towards the Good, and the two towards Evil; the one would be free, the two cling to servitude. If the two be overcome, there remains a bulwark of defence for them and for their master; but if the one be the weaker, it is drawn away by the two, and punished in this life here below. It is this one, my son, which ought to be thy guide. See that thou anoint thyself with oil for the struggle, maintain the fight for life, and remain victorious.

And now, my son, I am about to sum up our principles; thou wilt understand my words by remembering that which thou hast learnt.

All beings are endowed with motion; non-being alone is motionless. All bodies transform themselves some only decompose. All creatures are not mortal nor are all immortal. That which is dissoluble is corruptible; that which is permanent is immutable; that which is immutable is eternal; that which is continually generated is continually corrupted, but that which is born but once is not corrupted and is not changed into any other thing. First God, then the Universe, and thirdly Man; the Universe for Man, and Man for God. The emotional part of the Soul is mortal; her rational part is immortal; all substance is immortal, all substance is subjected to change. All being is dual; no being is permanent. All things are not animated by soul, but all that is being is animated by soul. All that is passive is sentient; all that is sentient is transient. Everything that suffers and enjoys is a mortal creature; all that enjoys and suffers not is a being immortal. Not every body is subject to disease, but every body so subject is destructible. In God is Intelligence; in Man is Reason. Reason is in Intelligence, Intelligence is intransient. There is nothing real in the corporeal; nothing false in the incorporeal. Everything that is born changes, but not everything born corrupts. There is nothing perfect upon earth, nor anything evil in heaven. God is perfect; man is evil. The good comes by will; evil against will. The Gods chose the good as good. Time is divine; law is human. Evil is the pabulum of the world; Time is the destruction of man. All things in heaven are immutable; nothing is immutable on earth. In heaven, then, is no servitude; on earth there is no freedom. Nothing in heaven is unknown; on earth nothing is known. There is nothing in common between celestial things and things terrestrial. All is irreproachable in heaven; on earth nothing is without reproach. The immortal knows no mortality; nor does the mortal know immortality. That which is sown does not always come up; but that which comes up has always been sown. Corruptible bodies have two periods of existence: from conception to birth, and from birth to death; but the eternal entity has one period only from the moment of being. Dissoluble bodies increase and diminish. Dissoluble matter divides itself according to two contrary terms - destruction and birth; immortal substance divides itself either into itself or into its similars. The birth of man is a destruction; the destruction of man is an element of birth. That which ends begins; that which begins ends. Among beings, some are in bodies, some in forms, some in energies. The body is in forms; form and energy are in bodies. The immortal receives nothing from the mortal; but the mortal receives from the immortal. The mortal enters not into an immortal form; but the immortal enters into a mortal body. Energies tend not upward, but downward. That which is on earth profits not that which is in heaven; but all that is in heaven profits that which is on earth. Heaven contains immortal entities; earth contains perishable bodies. Earth is irrational; heaven is reasonable. Celestial things are under the power of heaven; terrestrial things are upon earth. Heaven is the primordial element. Divine providence is order; necessity is the instrument with which providence works. Fortuity is the vehicle of disorder, the false image of energy, a delusive seeming. What is God but immutable Good, or man but continual evil?

In remembering these principles, thou wilt easily recollect the things I have explained to thee more at length, and which are therein resumed. But avoid speaking of them to the multitude; not that I desire to prohibit the multitude from knowing these things, but that I would not have thee exposed to the mockeries of the vulgar. Like attracts like; but between dissimilars there is no fellowship. These discourses ought to have but a small number of auditors, else before long they will have none at all. There is, moreover, a special peril attaching to them, for by means of them the wicked may be instigated to do worse. Keep thyself, therefore, from the crowd, which cannot understand the virtue of these discourses.

Tatios.
What meanest thou, my father?
Trismegistos.
Hearken, my son. The human race is drawn to-wards evil. Evil is its nature, and pleases it. If men should learn that the world is created, that all is done according to providence and necessity, and that by necessity and destiny all things are governed, they would readily begin to despise all things because they are created; to attribute vice to destiny, and to give the rein to all manner of iniquity. Therefore, abstain from the crowd, so that by means of ignorance the vulgar may be kept within bounds, even through fear of the unknown.

Footnotes

1 With Plato, says Dr. Menard, Trismegistos here opposes Intelligence, the first part of the Soul, to the two other parts, Passion and Desire.

PART II

Tatios.

Thou hast well explained to me these things, my father, but instruct me yet again concerning this. Thou hast told me that know-ledge and art are activities of the reason; and now thou sayest that brute animals are so called because they have no reason. Whence it must necessarily follow that they have neither knowledge nor art.

Trismegistos.

It necessarily so follows, my son.

Tatios.

How then is it, father, that we behold certain animals making use of scientific and constructive knowledge; as, for instance, the ants who store up provisions for the winter, the birds who devise nests, the cattle who know their stables and return thither?

Trismegistos.

It is neither science nor art that directs them, my son, but nature. Science and art are acquired, but these creatures have acquired nothing. That which is naturally performed is the product of the universal activity; science and art belong only to those who have acquired them. Functions which are the common heritage are natural functions. Thus, all men can make use of their eyes, but not all are musicians, archers, hunters, and so forth. Some only among the many learn a science or an art, and exercise it. If in like manner certain ants only did what other ants do not, then thou mightest say with reason that they possess the science or the art of storing provisions. But all act in the same way under the impulsion of Nature and without deliberate intent; whence it is evident that neither science nor art directs them.

Activities, O Tatios, are incorporeal, and are exercised in the body and by the body. Insomuch as they are incorporeal, thou mayest indeed call them immortal; insomuch as they cannot be exercised but by means of a body, I say that they are always in a body. That of which the end and cause are determined by providence and necessity cannot remain inactive. That which is shall still be, therein is its body and its life. For which reason there will always be bodies; wherefore the creation of bodies is an eternal function. For terrestrial bodies are corruptible; nevertheless, bodies are necessary as abodes and as instruments for the energies. Now, the energies are immortal, and that which is immortal is always active. The creation of bodies is, then, a function, and an eternal function.

The energies or faculties of the soul are not all at once manifest; certain of them are manifest from the time of the birth of man, in the non-rational part of his soul; and as the reasonable part develops itself with age, the loftier faculties also lend their assistance. The faculties are attached to bodies. They descend from divine forms into mortal forms, and by them bodies are

created. Each of the faculties exercises a function either of the body or of the soul, but they subsist in the soul independently of the body. For the energies are eternal, but the soul is not always imprisoned in a mortal body. She can live without it, yet the faculties cannot manifest themselves unless in a body. This, my son, is an arcane discourse. The body cannot remain without the soul, but being can.

Tatios.

What meanest thou, my father?

Trismegistos.

Understand me, O Tatios. When the soul is separated from the body, the body indeed remains, but it is undermined by interior dissolution, and ends by disintegrating. Such an effect cannot be produced without an active cause; therefore, there remains some energy in the body after the withdrawal of the soul. Between an immortal entity and a mortal entity there is this difference: that the first is formed of simple substance, but not so the second. One is active, the other passive. All active being dominates, all passive being obeys; one is free, and governs; the other is in servitude, and subject to impulsion.

Now, the energies are not only in animate bodies, but in inanimate, such as wood, stone, and other like things. By means of the energies these things increase, fructify, ripen, decompose, dissolve, putrefy, disintegrate, and undergo all those changes of which inanimate bodies are susceptible. For energy is that which produces change, or becoming. And becoming is multiple, or rather universal. Never will anything capable of birth be wanting to the universe, because beings are continually brought forth by it and continually destroyed. All energy is then indestructible, no matter of what nature or in what body it is manifest. But among the energies, some are exerted in divine entities, some in mortal entities; some are universal, others special; some act upon species, others on individuals pertaining to these. Divine energies are exerted in eternal entities, and are perfect as these. Partial energies act by means of living beings; special energies in everything which exists. Whence it results, my son, that the whole universe is full of energies. For since energies necessarily manifest in bodies, there are many bodies in the universe. Nevertheless, the energies are more numerous than the bodies, for often there exist one, two, three energies in a body, without counting those which are universally distributed. I call those universal energies which are inseparable from bodies and which manifest themselves by sensations and movements, and without which no body could exist. Far otherwise are those special energies which manifest themselves in human minds by art, science, and labour. The sensations accompany the energies, or rather are the consequence of these last.

Understand, O my son, the difference there is between the energies and the sensations. Energy comes from above; sensation is of the body, and from the body has its being. It is the seat of the energy, which manifests by means of it, and from which it obtains, as it were, a vehicle. For this reason I say that sensations are corporeal and mortal; their existence is bound up with that of the body, they are born therewith, and therewith they die. Immortal energies have not sensation, precisely because of the nature of their essence; for there can be no other sensation than that of some good or some evil which happens to a body or which departs therefrom, and immortal entities are not subject to these accidents.

Tatios.
Sensation, then, is experienced by all bodies?
Trismegistos.
Yes, my son, and in all bodies the energies act.
Tatios.
Even in inanimate bodies, my father?
Trismegistos.
Even in inanimate bodies. Sensations are of different kinds; those of reasonable beings are accompanied by reason; those of beings without reason are purely corporeal; those of inanimate beings are passive, and consist only in growth and decay. Starting from one principle and arriving at one end, passion and sensation are alike the product of the energies. In animate beings, there are two other energies which accompany the passions and the sensations - to wit, joy and sorrow. Without these, the animated being, and, above all, the reasonable being, would feel nothing; they may then be considered as modes of the affections in reasonable beings, or indeed in all living beings. They are activities manifested by the sensations, corporeal movements produced by the irrational parts of the soul. Joy and sorrow are alike evil; for joy - that is, the sensation accompanied by pleasure - draws after it great evils; sorrow, likewise, involves penalties and suffering, yet more severe. Both joy and sorrow, then, are evil.

Tatios.
Is sensation the same thing in the soul and in the body, my father?
Trismegistos.
What meanest thou, my child, by the sensation of the soul?
Tatios.
The soul is truly incorporeal. But sensation is as a body, my father, for it

exists in a body.

Trismegistos.

If we place it in the body, my son, we indeed assimilate it either to the soul or to the energies, which, although in the body, are incorporeal. But sensation is neither an energy nor a soul, nor anything distinct from the body; it is not, therefore, incorporeal. If it be not incorporeal, it must necessarily be corporeal, for there is nothing which is neither corporeal nor incorporeal.

PART III

The Lord, the Creator of immortal forms, O Tatios, after having accomplished His work, made nothing further, nor does He now make anything. Once consigned to themselves and united to one another, these eternal forms move without having need of anything; or if, indeed, they are necessary one to another, they have at least no need of any extraneous impulsion, since they are immortal. Such ought, indeed, to be the nature of the creations of the supreme God. But our (immediate) maker has a body; he has brought us forth, and unceasingly he brings forth, and will bring forth dissoluble and mortal bodies, for he ought not to imitate his own Creator, and, moreover, he cannot. For the first has evolved His creations from His own essence, primordial and incorporeal; the second has formed us of that which is corporeal and engendered. Whence it follows naturally, that heavenly forms born of incorporeal essence are imperishable, while our bodies, being constituted of corporeal matter, are consequently weak in themselves, and need extraneous assistance.

For how, indeed, could the combination which composes our bodies be sustained, if it were not continually fed and supported by elements of the same nature? The earth, the water, the fire, and the air flow into us and renew our covering. We are so weak that we cannot even endure a single day of movement. Thou knowest well, my son, that without the repose of the night our bodies would not resist the day's toil. For this reason our good creator, in his universal providence, has ensured the continual life of his creatures by devising sleep, the restorer of movement, and by assigning to repose an equal or even longer time (than to labour). Meditate, my son, on this virtue of sleep, opposed to that of the soul, and not less energetic. For if the function of the soul be movement, bodies cannot live without slumber, which loosens and unbinds the yoke of the organism, and by its restoring action dispenses to it the matter which it needs, giving water to the blood, earth to the bones, air to the nerves and vessels, fire to the eyes. And hence the great pleasure which the body finds in sleep.

[NOTE. - The opening passage of this fragmentary discourse will not lead the reader into error if he bears in mind the pantheistic character of all Hermetic teaching. The influx of the divine substance into the universe is perpetual, but the channels or forms through which it flows are immutable, unchangeable, and self-sustaining. The method of nature is determined from the beginning, and is incapable of variation or of intermittance. But the descent of soul into generation is a continual process, and will not cease until the creative period or "Day of Manifestation" closes. There has never been any suspension of the divine energies since the commencement of their primordial operation. The outflow of Being into Existence is unending, otherwise natural generation would cease, and evolution be arrested. The secondary creator mentioned in this fragment is the Demiourgos, the fabricator of the material universe.]

A.K.

PART IV

Great and divine power is established, O my son, in the midst of the universe, beholding all that is done by men upon earth. In the divine order all is governed by providential Necessity; among men the same function belongs to Justice. The first of these governments includes celestial things, for the Gods neither will, nor can, transgress; not being subject to error, which is the source of sin, they are sinless. The second, Justice, is charged to correct, upon earth, the evil which happens among men. The human race, being mortal, and formed of corruptible matter, is subject to fall away when the sight of divine things does not sustain it (in virtue). Herein Justice exerts its action. By means of the energies which he draws from Nature, man is subject to Destiny; by the errors of his life, to Justice.

PART V

Here, then, is that which can be said of the three tenses. They are not by themselves, and they are not bound together; again, they are bound together and are by themselves. Can the present be supposed without the existence of the past? One cannot exist without another, for the present is generated by the past, and from the present the future comes forth. If we wish to go to the root of the matter, we must reason thus: - The past tense is withdrawn into that which no longer is; the future is not so long as it has not become present; the present, in its turn, ceases to be itself the instant that it remains. Can that which does not endure for an instant and which has no fixed centre be called present when it cannot even be said to exist? Moreover, since the past is indistinguishable from the present, and the present from the future, they become one. There is among them identity, unity, continuity. Therefore time is continuous and divisible, even while it is one and identical.

PART VI

O my son, matter becomes; formerly it was, for matter is the vehicle of becoming.[1] Becoming is the mode of activity of the uncreate and foreseeing God. Having been endowed with the germ of becoming, matter is brought into birth, for the creative force fashions it according to the ideal forms. Matter not yet engendered, had no form; it becomes when it is put into operation.

Footnotes

1 Dr. Menard observes that in Greek, the same word signifies to be born and to become. The idea here is that the material of the world is in its essence eternal, but that before creation or "becoming," it is in a passive and motionless condition. Thus it "was" before being "put into operation;" now, it "becomes," that is, it is mobile and progressive. Creation is thus the period of activity of God, who, according to Hermetic thought, has two modes - Activity, or existence, God evolved (Deus explicitus); and Passivity of Being - God involved (Deus implicitus). Both modes are perfect and complete, as are the waking and sleeping states of man. Fichte, the German philosopher, distinguished Being (Seyn) as One, which we know only through existence (Daseyn) as the Manifold. This view is thoroughly Hermetic. The "Ideal Forms," mentioned in the above fragment, are the archetypal or formative ideas of the Neo-Platonists; the eternal and subjective concepts of things subsisting in the Divine Mind prior to "creation" or "becoming."

A.K.

PART VII

To speak of the Real with certainty, O Tatios, is an impossible thing to man, himself an imperfect creature, composed of imperfect parts, and constituted of an assemblage of foreign particles; nevertheless, as much as it is possible and permissible to me, I affirm that Reality is only in eternal beings, the forms of which also are real. Fire is but fire and no more; earth is nothing else than earth; air is only air. Put our bodies are compounded of all these; we have in us fire, earth, water, and air, which yet are neither fire, nor earth, nor water, nor air, nor anything truly. If, then, from the beginning Reality is foreign to our constitution, how shall we behold Reality, or speak thereof, or even understand it, unless indeed by the Will of God? Mundane things, O Tatios, are not then themselves real, but the simulacra of Reality, and not all are even such; some are but illusion and error, O Tatios, fantastic appearances, mere phantoms. When such an appearance receives an influx from above, then, indeed, it becomes a similitude of the Real, but without this superior influence it remains an illusion. In the same way a portrait is a painted image of a body, but not the body it represents. It appears to have eyes, but sees nothing; ears, but hears nothing; and so on of the rest of it. It is an image which deceives the sight; it appears a reality, and is but a shadow. Those who behold not the False behold the True; if, then, we understand and see everything as it truly is, we see the Real; but if we see that which is not, we can neither understand nor know anything of the Real.

Tatios.

There is, then, my father, a Real even upon earth?

Trismegistos.

Reality is not upon the earth, my son, and it cannot be thereon, but it can be comprehended by a few men to whom God vouchsafes the divine vision. Nothing on earth is real, there are only appearances and opinions on earth; yet all is real for intelligence and reason. Wherefore to think and to speak the truth this indeed may be called real.

Tatios.

What sayest thou? It is right to think and speak that which truly is, and yet nothing is true upon earth?

Trismegistos.

This certainly is true, that we know nothing of Truth. How should it be otherwise, my son? Truth is the supreme virtue, the sovereign Good which is not obscured by matter, nor circumscribed by the body; the naked Good, evident, unalterable, august, immutable. Now, the things which are here below thou seest, my son, are incompatible with the Good; they are perishable, changing, various, passing from form to form. That which is not even identical with itself, how can it be real? All that transforms itself is illusive, not only in itself, but by the appearances which it presents to us one after another.

Tatios.

Is not even man real, my father?

Trismegistos.

He is not real, my son, as man. The real consists solely in itself, and remains what it is. Man is composed of manifold elements, and does not continue identical with himself. So long as he inhabits a body he passes from one age to another, and from one form to another. Often, after but a short interval of time, parents no longer are able to recognize their children, nor children their parents. That which changes in such wise as to be no longer recognizable as itself, can it be a real thing, Tatios? Should we not rather think this succession of diverse appearances an illusion? Look only on the eternal and the Good as the Real. Man is transient, therefore he is not real; he is but appearance, and appearance is the supreme illusion.

Tatios.

Then the celestial bodies themselves are not real, my father, since they also vary.

Trismegistos.

That which is subject to birth and to change is not real, but the works of the great Father may receive from Him a real substance. Nevertheless, there is in them a certain falsity, seeing that they too are variable, for nothing is real save that which is identical with itself.

Tatios.

What, then, may we call indeed real, my father?

Trismegistos.

The sun, the only one of all creatures that changes not, and which remains the same. For this reason is confided to him alone the ordinance of the universe; he is the chief and the maker of everything; I venerate him and prostrate myself before his truth, and, after the first Unity, I recognize in him the creator.

Tatios.

And what, then, is the primordial Reality, O my father?

Trismegistos.

He Who is One and alone, O Tatios; He Who is not made of matter, nor in any body, Who has neither colour nor form, Who changes not, nor is transmuted, but who always Is.

That which is illusion is perishable, my son. The providence of the Real has limited and will limit by dissolution all mundane things, for dissolution is the condition of all births; all that is brought forth dissolves in order to be again brought forth. It is necessary that out of dissolution life should come into existence, and that life in its turn should decay, in order that the generation of creatures should never cease. Behold, then, in this perpetual birth, the Creator before all! Creatures born of dissolution are but shadows, they become at one time this, at another that; for they cannot be the same, and how is it possible for that which is not identical with itself, to be a real thing? Such must then, my son, be called appearances, and man must be regarded as an appearance of Humanity; as, also, a child is an appearance of childhood, a young man of adolescence, an adult of manhood, an old man of senility. For how shall it be said that a man is a man, a child a child, a youth a youth, a grown man a grown man, an old man an old man, since by incessant transformations they deceive us both as to what they were, and what they have become? Behold, then, in all these things, my son, only the illusive appearances of a superior Reality; and since, indeed, this is the case, I define Illusion as the expression of the Real.

PART VIII

To understand God is difficult; to speak of God, impossible. For the corporeal cannot express the incorporeal; the imperfect cannot comprehend the perfect. How is the eternal to be associated with the transient? The first abides for ever, the other is fleeting; the first is the Real, the other is a reflected shadow. As much as weakness differs from strength, or smallness from greatness, so much the mortal differs from the divine. The distance which divides them one from the other obscures the vision of the beautiful. Bodies are visible to sight, and that which the eye beholds the tongue is able to express. But that which has not any body, nor appearance, nor form, nor matter, cannot be apprehended by sense.

I understand, O Tatios, I understand that which it is impossible to define - that is God.

[The above fragments are from the "Physical Eclogues" and "Florilegium" of Stobæus.]

FRAGMENTS of the WRITINGS of HERMES to AMMON.

PART I

That which rules the universe is Providence; that which contains the universe and limits it is Necessity; Destiny impels and enfolds all things by the compulsory force which belongs thereto. It is Destiny which is the cause of birth and of the dissolution of Life. The universe, then, first receives Providence, the first ordained. Providence extends to the skies, about which the Gods revolve, in perpetual and untiring motion. There is Destiny because there is Necessity. Providence foresees, Destiny determines, the position of the stars. Such is the universal law.

PART II

All things are produced by Nature and Destiny, nor is any place void of Providence. Providence is the Free Will of the Supreme God; whence two spontaneous forces, Necessity and Destiny. Destiny is subject to Providence and to Necessity; and to Destiny are subject the stars. Therefore, no man can escape from Destiny, nor arm himself against the action of the stars. For they are the instruments of Destiny; by their means the will of Destiny is accomplished throughout all Nature and in human existence. [1]

Footnotes

1 I commend the above fragments to the careful consideration of Hermetists. Many persons find it difficult to reconcile belief in the "ruling of the stars" with belief in free will. At first sight it appears unjust and arbitrary that certain lines of life - even vicious ones - should be indicated by the "rulers of nativities" as the only lines in which the "native" will prosper; and they ask incredulously whether it can be rationally supposed that the "accident" of the day and hour of birth, is, by Divine Providence, permitted to direct and dominate the whole career of an intelligent and responsible being. But this objection is superficial, and the result of incomplete knowledge. For the difficulties of astrological science, if viewed in the light of Karmic Predestination or Fate, not only disappear, but give place to the unfoldment of a most lucid and admirable system of responsible causation. There is but

one hypothesis capable of solving the enigma of Fate, and that hypothesis is a doctrine common to all the greater schools of thought - Vedic, Buddhist, Kabbalistic, Hermetic, Platonic, - the hypothesis, to wit, of multiple existences, or the doctrine of the Metempsychosis. Destiny, in the view of these philosophies, is not arbitrary, but acquired. Every man makes his own Fate; and nothing is truer than the saying that "Character is Destiny." For that which in one existence is Will, becomes in the next Fate. By the hands of men themselves, then, are their natal lines cast, whether in pleasant and virtuous, or in painful and vicious paths. For in what manner soever an ego conducts itself in one existence, by that conduct, by that order of thought and habit it builds for itself its destiny in a future existence. And the ego is enchained by these pre-natal influences, and by them irresistibly compelled into a new nativity at the time of such conjunction of planets and signs as oblige it into certain courses, or incline it strongly thereto. Hence "Destiny," or Karma, is said by Hermes to "determine the position of the stars." And if the course so defined be evil, and the ruling such as to favour chiefly vicious propensities, the afflicted ego, even though assuredly reaping the just effects of its own demerit, is not left without a remedy. For the ego may oppose its will to the stellar ruling, and heroically adopt a course opposed to the direction of the natal influences. Thereby, indeed, the ego may bring itself under a curse for such period as those influences have power, for, as Hermes tells us, "no man can escape from Destiny, nor preserve himself from the action of the stars;" but at the same time, the will thus exerted will reverse the planetary affinities acquired, and give a new "set" to the current of the Karmic predestination, so that the ruling signs of the next nativity will be favourable to virtue and to a loftier state. But the "stars" and "stellar influences" which are thus the "instruments of Destiny" are immediately microcosmic, and only mediately macrocosmic. (For the full exposition and interpretation of this important subject, the reader is referred to "Astrology Theologized," now about to be republished in the present series of Occult Reprints, by Robt. H. Fryar, Bath.)

A.K.

PART III

The soul is, then, an incorporeal essence, and even when she is in a body, she does not wholly lose her manner of being. Her essence is that of perpetual movement, the spontaneous movement of thought; yet is she not moved in any thing else, nor towards any thing else, nor for any thing else. For she is a primordial force, and that which is primal needs not that which is secondary. The expression "in any thing" is applicable to place, to time, to nature;

"towards any thing" is applicable to a harmony, to a form, to a figure; "for any thing" is applicable to the body, because time, place, nature, and form are related to the body. All these terms are conjoined by reciprocal bonds. The body requires place, for it is not possible to conceive of a body unless also of a place occupied by it; a body changes its nature, such change is not possible unless in time, and by means of movement in nature; nor can the component parts of a body be united unless by harmony of form. Space exists on account of corporeity, it contains the changes thereof and suffers it not to be annihilated in these changes. The body passes from one condition to another, but in quitting its first condition it ceases not to be body, it takes only another condition. It was body, it remains body, its state alone varies; wherefore, that which changes in corporeity is quality and mode of being. Place, time, and natural movement, themselves bodiless, have each their special property. The property of space is to contain; the property of time is interval and number; the property of nature is movement; the property of harmony is affinity; the property of body is change; the property of soul is thought.

PART IV

The soul is then an incorporeal essence; if she had a body she would be unable to preserve herself, for every body has need of breath and of life which consists in order. Wherever there is birth there is fluxion. To "become" presupposes magnitude, that is augmentation; augmentation involves diminution, which, in turn, brings about destruction. That which receives the form of life participates in being by means of the soul. In order to produce existence, it is necessary to exist; existence I define to be a reasonable becoming and participation in intelligent life. Life constitutes the creature, intelligence renders it reasonable, the body makes it mortal. The soul is then incorporeal, and possesses an immutable force. Can an intelligent creature exist without a living essence? Can he be rational if an intelligent essence does not maintain in him rational life? If intelligence does not manifest itself in all creatures, it is on account of the constitution of the body in regard to harmony. If heat dominates in the constitution thereof, the creature is volatile and ardent; if cold dominates, it is heavy and slow. Nature distributes the elements of the body according to a law of harmony. This harmonic combination has three forms: - the hot, the cold, and the temperate. Conjunction is established according to stellar influence. The soul appropriates the body destined to her, and causes it to live by the operation of nature. Nature assimilates the harmony of bodies to the disposition of the stars, and the combination of their elements to the harmony of the stars; so that there may be reciprocal sympathy. For the purpose of stellar harmony is to engender sympathies in agreement with Destiny.

PART V

The soul is then, O Ammon, an essence having its end in itself, receiving from the beginning the life prepared for her, and attracting to herself, as a material, a certain reason endowed with passion and desire. Passion is a matter; if it enters into accord with the intelligent part of the soul, it becomes courage, and does not yield to fear. Desire also is a matter; in association with the rational part of the soul, it becomes aspiration and yields not to voluptuousness. For reason enlightens the blindness of desire. When the faculties of the soul are thus co-ordinated under the supremacy of reason, they produce justice. The government of the faculties of the soul belongs to the Intellectual Principle which subsists in itself in its provident reason, having for authority its own reason. It governs all like a magistrate; its provident reason serves it as counsellor. The reason of this Principle is the cognizance of the reasons which furnish the image of rationality to the irrational; an image relatively obscure when compared with reason, but rational when compared to the irrational, as an echo compared to a voice, or the light of the moon compared to that of the sun. Passion and desire are ordained according to a certain reason; they mutually attract each other, and establish between them a circulatory current of thought. Every soul is immortal, and always in movement. For we have seen that movements proceed either from energies or from bodies. We have seen, also, that the soul, being incorporeal, proceeds not from any matter, but from an essence incorporeal itself. Everything that is born is necessarily produced by some other thing. Two movements necessarily accompany everything the generation of which involves decay; that of the soul which moves it, and that of the body which augments, diminishes, and decomposes it, in decomposing itself. It is thus that I define the movement of perishable bodies. But the soul is perpetually in motion, without cessation she moves and produces movement. Thus every soul is immortal and always in motion, moved by her own activity. There are three species in souls: divine, human, and irrational. The divine soul abides in a divine form, it is therein that she has her energy; therein she moves and acts. When this soul separates herself from mortal creatures, she forsakes her irrational parts and enters into the divine form; and, as she is always in motion, she is borne along in the universal movement. The human soul has also something divine, but she is bound to irrational elements desire and passion; these elements are undying, because they are energies; but they are energies of mortal bodies, therefore they are removed from the divine part of the soul, which inhabits the divine form. When this divine part enters into a mortal body and meets therein these irrational elements, she becomes, by means of their presence, a human soul. The soul of animals is composed of passion and desire, therefore the animals are called brutes, because their soul is deprived of reason. The fourth species in soul, that possessed by inanimate creatures, is placed outside the bodies actuated. This soul moves in the divine form, and impels it passively.[1]

Footnotes

1 The above fragment appears to me extremely obscure and unsatisfactory. I include it in the series of Hermetic writings because it is quoted as such by Stobæus, but it certainly needs much interpretation and explanation, if it be indeed genuine.
        A.K.

PART VI

The soul is, then, an eternal and intelligent essence; having for thought her own reason. She enters into association with the concept of harmony. Separated from the physical body, she endures in herself, she is independent in the Ideal world. She controls her reason, and confers on the entity emerging into life a movement analogous to her own thought, that is being; for the property of the soul is to assimilate other things to her own character. There are two kinds of vital movement: the one conform-able to the essence of the soul, the other to the nature of the body. The first is general, the second particular; the first is independent, the second is subject to necessity. For everything moved is subject to the necessary law of the mover. But the motor movement is united by affinity to the intelligent principle. It behoves the soul to be incorporeal, and to be essentially different from the physical body, for if she had a body she would have neither reason nor thought. All bodies are unintelligent, but in receiving the spirit they become animated and breathe. The breath belongs to the body, but reason contemplates the beauty of the essential. The sensible spirit discerns appearances. It is distributed into organic sensations; mental perception is a part of it, as also is the acoustic, olfactive, gustative, and tactile sense. This spirit, attracted by thought, discerns sensations, otherwise it creates only phantoms, for it belongs to the body, and receives all things. The reason of the essential is the judgment. To the reason belongs the cognizance of lofty things; but to the sensible spirit, opinion. This last receives its energy from the external world; but the former from within itself.

[The foregoing fragments are from the "Physical Eclogues" of Stobæus.]

VARIOUS HERMETIC FRAGMENTS

PART I

There are, then, essential spirit, reason, intelligence, perception. Opinion and sensation tend towards perception, reason towards the essential spirit; thought advances independently. Thought is associated with perception. Conjoined, all these become a single form, which is that of the soul. Opinion and sensation tend also towards perfection, but they do not continue in the same condition, they exhibit excess, failure, or variation. Separated from perception, they deteriorate; approximating to and following it, they participate in the intellectual reason through the sciences. We have the power of choice; it depends on us to choose either the best or the worst by our will. The choice of evil approximates us to the corporeal nature, and subjects us to Destiny. The intellectual spirit which is in us, being free, the intellectual reason is free also, always identical with itself, and independent of Destiny. Therefore, in following this higher and intelligent reason, ordained by the supreme God, the spirit is superior to the order of Nature over creatures; but the soul which attaches herself to these creatures participates in their destiny, though foreign to their nature.[1]

Footnotes

1 In the above fragment the power of the human will is clearly asserted as the only instrument by which Destiny may be controlled. By continued and ardent striving towards the purely spiritual and intelligent, the soul frees herself from the power of Destiny (Karma), and at length passes into beatitude. She transcends natural order, and enters into the divine. This is Saintship. Inversely, by attaching herself to sensible things, and by suffering herself to be borne away by passion and desire towards illusory existence, she becomes caught on the ever-rolling wheel of Destiny, and made subject to the order of Nature, which is that of Metamorphosis. Whereas her true duty and happiness are to aspire continually upwards, addressing herself by means of purified passion and desire towards the One, and away from the Manifold.

A.K.

PART II

There is, then, a state of Being superior to all beings, and to all that actually is. Being is that by which universal essentiality is common to all intelligible entities actually existing... Nature is sensible essentiality, including in itself all sensible objects. Midway are the intellectual and sensible gods. The concepts of intelligence are related to the intellectual gods, the concepts of opinion to the sensible gods, which are reflexions of the intelligences; as, for instance, the sun is the image of the creative and celestial God. For as God has created the universe, so the sun creates animals, produces plants, and governs fluid things.

[These fragments are from Stobæus' Eclogues, "Physical and Moral."]

PART III

Wherefore the incorporeal vision comes forth from the body to contemplate beauty, lifting itself up and adoring, not the form, nor the body, nor the appearance, but that which, behind all, is calm, tranquil, substantial, immutable; that which is all, alone and one, that which is by itself and in itself, similar to itself, and without variation.

PART IV

If thou understandest this one and only Good, thou wilt find nothing impossible, for all virtue is therein. Think not that this Good is in anyone, nor that it is outside of anyone. It is without limit, being the limit of all. Nothing contains it, it contains all in itself. For what distinction is there between the corporeal and the incorporeal, the create and the uncreate; that which is subject to necessity and that which is free; between terrestrial things and things celestial, corruptible things and things eternal? Is it not that these subsist freely, and that those are subject to the bondage of necessity? That which is below is imperfect and perishable.

PART V

Beneath nature and the ideal world is placed the pyramid. Its corner stone, placed on its summit, is the Creative Word of the universal Lord, which, after Him, is the first Power, uncreate, infinite, begotten of Him and antecedent to all His creations. He is the offspring of the Most Perfect, the fruitful and true Son. The nature of this intelligent Word is a generating and productive nature. Call it as thou wilt - generation, or nature, or character. But think this only, that he is perfect in the Perfect, and issued from the Perfect, that all his works are perfectly good, and that he is the source of creation and of life. Since such is his nature, he is well named.

. . . . .

But for the providence of the Lord of the universe Who causes me to reveal these words, you would not have so great a desire to seek out such matters. Now, therefore, hear the end of this discourse. This Spirit of whom I have so often spoken is necessary to all; for he maintains all, he gives life to all, he nourishes all. He outflows from the holy Source, and without ceasing comes to the aid of spirits and to all living creatures.

[The foregoing are from Cyril.]

PART VI

"Thus the Ideal Light was before the Ideal Light, and the luminous Intelligence of Intelligence was always, and its unity was nothing else than the Spirit enveloping the universe. Out of Whom is neither God, nor Angels, nor any other essentials, for He is the Lord of all things and the power and the light; and all depends on Him and is in Him. His perfect Word, generative and creative, descending into generative Nature and into generating water, rendered the water fruitful."

Having thus spoken, he rose and said: - "I adjure thee, Heaven, holy work of the great God; I adjure thee, Voice of the Father, uttered in the beginning when the universal world was framed; I adjure thee by the Word, only Son of the Father Who upholds all things; be favorable, be favorable!"

[The above fragment is cited by Suidas.]

PART VII

Seven Planets revolve in the ways of Olympos, and by them Eternity is measured: - The Moon which illumines the night, the gloomy Kronos, the gentle Sun, the Paphian Goddess, protectress of marriage, the valiant Ares, the fruitful Hermes, and Zeus the principle of birth and the fount of nature. These, likewise, have received the human race in heritage; and there are, within us, the Moon, Zeus, Ares, Aphrodite, Kronos, Phoebus, Hermes. Moreover, we draw from the etherial fluid our tears, our laughter, our wrath, our speech, our generation, our sleep, our desire. Tears are of Kronos, generation of Zeus, speech of Hermes, valour of Ares, sleep of Artemis, desire of Kytheræa (Aphrodite), laughter of Apollo, for he it is who pours joy upon human thought and on the infinite world.

[This fragment, cited by Stobæus, is in verse, and Heeren supposes it to be part of an Orphic hymn. It is thoroughly Hermetic, and its recognition of Man as the epitome and reflex of the universe is entirely in accord also with Kabbalistic teaching. - A.K.]

PART VIII

Hermes affirms that those who know God, are preserved from assaults of the evil one, and are not even subject to Destiny. The knowledge of God is religion.

[From Lactantius: "Divine Institutions."]

THE END

Parchment Books is committed to publishing high quality
Esoteric/Occult classic texts at a reasonable price.

With the premium on space in modern dwellings, we also strive - within the limits of good book design - to make our products as slender as possible, allowing more books to be fitted into a given bookshelf area.

Parchment Books is an imprint of Aziloth Books, which has established itself as a publisher boasting a diverse list of powerful, quality titles, including novels of flair and originality, and factual publications on controversial issues that have not found a home in the rather staid and politically-correct atmosphere of many publishing houses.

Titles Include:

Secret Doctrines of the Rosicrucians	Magus Incognito
Corpus Hermeticum	(trans. GRS Mead)
The Virgin of the World	Hermes Trismegistus
Raja Yoga	Yogi Ramacharaka
Theosophy	Rudolf Steiner
The Most Holy Trinosophia	St Germain
The Gospel of Thomas	Anonymous
Pistis Sophia	(trans. GRS Mead)
The Siugnature of All Things	Jacob Boehme

Obtainable at all good online and local bookstores. View Aziloth's full list at:

www.azilothbooks.com

We are a small, approachable company and would love to hear any of your comments and suggestions on our plans, products, or indeed on absolutely anything. Aziloth is also interested in hearing from aspiring authors whom we might publish. We look forward to meeting you. Contact us at:

info@azilothbooks.com.

CATHEDRAL CLASSICS

Parchment Book's sister imprint, Cathedral Classics hosts an array of classic literature, from ancient tomes to twentieth-century masterpieces, all of which deserve a place in your home. A small selection is detailed below:

Mary Shelley	*Frankenstein*
H G Wells	*The Time Machine; The Invisible Man*
Niccolo Machiavelli	*The Prince*
Omar Khayyam	*The Rubaiyat of Omar Khayyam*
Joseph Conrad	*Heart of Darkness; The Secret Agent*
Jane Austen	*Persuasion; Northanger Abbey*
Oscar Wilde	*The Picture of Dorian Gray*
Voltaire	*Candide*
Bulwer Lytton	*The Coming Race*
Arthur Conan Doyle	*The Adventures of Sherlock Holmes*
John Buchan	*The Thirty-Nine Steps*
Friedrich Nietzsche	*Beyond Good and Evil*
Henry James	*Washington Square*
Stephen Crane	*The Red Badge of Courage*
Ralph Waldo Emmerson	*Self-Reliance, and Other Essays, (series 1&2)*
Sun Tzu	*The Art of War*
Charles Dickens	*A Christmas Carol*
Fyodor Dostoyevsky	*The Gambler; The Double*
Virginia Wolf	*To the Lighthouse; Mrs Dalloway.*
Johann W Goethe	*The Sorrows of Young Werther*
Walt Whitman	*Leaves of Grass - 1855 edition*
Confucius	*Analects*
Anonymous	*Beowulf*
Anne Bronte	*Agnes Grey*
More	*Utopia*
Farid ud-Din Attar	*The Conference of Birds*

full list at: www.azilothbooks.com

Obtainable at all good online and local bookstores.

www.ingramcontent.com/pod-product-compliance
Lightning Source LLC
Chambersburg PA
CBHW070614050426
42450CB00011B/3053